George & Polly

Thanks for All your
Support and Friendship

John S Mercher

Great of Shindon
of

Charles Mercher 2019

Hamburger Dreams

Also by Christopher Carosa...

From Cradle to Retirement

 – The Child IRA: How to Start a Newborn Baby on the Road to Comfortable Retirement While Still in a Cozy Cradle

Hey! What's My Number?

 – How to Improve the Odds You Will Retire in Comfort

A Pizza The Action

 – Everything I Ever Learned About Business I Learned by Working in a Pizza Stand at the Erie County Fair

50 Hidden Gems of Greater Western New York

 – A Handbook for Those Too Proud to Believe "Wide Right" and "No Goal" Define Us

401(k) Fiduciary Solutions

 – Expert Guidance for 401(k) Plan Sponsors on How to Effectively and Safely Manage Plan Compliance and Investments by Sharing the Fiduciary Burden with Experienced Professionals

Hamburger Dreams

How Classic Crime Solving Techniques

Helped Crack the Case of

America's Greatest Culinary Mystery

by

Christopher Carosa

Pandamensional Solutions, Inc.

Mendon, New York

What Others Are Saying About Christopher Carosa's
Hamburger Dreams

"It gives me delight to report *Hamburger Dreams* is both scrupulously researched and written with graceful style. I could not put it down and finished it in a single sitting."

> ➤ Craig Shelton, James Beard Award Winning Chef, Shelton Hospitality Group

"The hamburger is the most American of sandwiches, and as such it's quite deserving of a definitive history tracing its 19th century roots. Chris Carosa has written the most detailed compendium of the birth and life of the American burger. He searched everywhere for primary sources and separated fact and fiction. His efforts have paid off. His book is one big triple cheese with everything on it."

> ➤ Dave Lieber, *The Dallas Morning News*

"As a dedicated, if decidedly amateur food historian, I have always been fascinated by the potential big bangs of some of our favorite dishes. None more so than the blessed hamburger. In *Hamburger Dreams* Chris Carosa has created the most savory of culinary whodunnits, using the techniques of modern crime solving to examine the four major 'suspects' who claim to have created the World's most famous sandwich. I won't give anything away, but suffice to say, after reading this book, you will never look at a hamburger in quite the same way ever again."

> ➤ Simon Majumdar, Author (*Eat My Globe*), Food and Travel Writer, Broadcaster, Podcaster

"*Hamburger Dreams* is a fascinating and well-researched account of the origin of the hamburger. Part culinary-mystery and part documentary, I thoroughly enjoyed both Chris Carosa's investigation and the delightful way in which it was presented."

> ➤ Liz Petty, Creator - culinarymysteries.net

"*Hamburger Dreams* is not only a culinary 'Whodunit,' but a 'How did he do that?'

Faced with a plethora of hamburger lore, conflicting primary resources, and multiple family descendants vying for claim to the global giant of popular foods, Chris Carosa masterfully unravels each clue to this food mystery with the brilliance of a culinary gumshoe and the diligence of a conscientious journalist.

Foodies will delight in the human side of hamburger's story and culinary historians will awe at Chris Carosa's scholarship.

Like all good mysteries, *Hamburger Dreams* is a real page-turner with a surprising conclusion."

> Pamela J. Vaccaro, Author, *Beyond the Ice Cream Cone: the whole scoop on food at the 1904 World's Fair*

"Chris Carosa is a born narrator who provides an immense amount of historical material with freshness and a sense of fun. It's hard to imagine the depth of his research. A personal note: reading *Hamburger Dreams* is almost as good as eating one."

> Lois Anne Rothert, Author, *The Soups of France*

"With meaty research and tantalizing story-telling, Carosa slices and dices through competing claims on America's most iconic sandwich. A foodie's whodunit, this book will keep you hungry to read straight through to the end."

> Dr. Beth Forrest, Food Historian and Professor at the Culinary Institute of America

For Kenny:
...because this really is all your fault

TABLE OF CONTENTS

FOREWORD

As a student you never stop learning the overwhelming history about Yale University, but; at some point during your first semester, you would be informed by one of your new classmates that, "That's Louie's Lunch. They invented the hamburger." WHAT?

This was not just another in an infinitely long list of historical facts that you would be exposed to in your early academic career. By the time you arrived on campus you would have become aware of previous alumni:

6 US Presidents,

18 Supreme Court Justices

50 US Senators,

20 Nobel Laureates,

30 Pulitzer Prize winners

And, just as you have begun to absorb the "small fish in a big pond" truth that, "you probably don't have what it takes to measure up", you begin to become aware of Yale traditions: That the *Yale Daily News* is the oldest daily collegiate newspaper in America; that The Whiffenpoofs, are the oldest collegiate a cappella group, formed in 1909; The Yale-Harvard football game, ("The Game") is the oldest Collegiate rivalry in America dating back to1875. And even older, the Yale-Harvard Crew Race "The Regatta" dates back to 1852.

Subsequently, you begin to learn of mysteries and lores more Illuminati-like than you would care to admit - of secret societies, of a skull of Geronimo, of rites of initiation, of numerological moments surrounding the number 322, and any last shred of the scholarship student's self-esteem would be tested sorely.

Names of the illustrious and rich history surround you at every turn. But the Hamburger? And its grand creator?

"Oh yes, that's Louie's Lunch – that's where the hamburger was invented" You feel a rush of redemptive inclusion. Here, at last a foothold for the ego. Something truly important happened here.

The 1974 *New York Times* story, "Burger 'Birthplace' Faces Bulldozer," seemed to transfigure the legend into facts - and that was that.

It could be easily forgiven if the Yale community might receive Chris Carosa's hamburger exposé as something of a class betrayal. Why disabuse us of a pleasant and easily swept-under-the-rug fiction. And then you remember that all of us in the hard sciences were initiated into the three pillars of scientific thinking: empiricism, rationalism, and skepticism. The practice of these leads to self-questioning and a willingness to change one's beliefs. And it was in that spirit that I was thrilled when Chris asked me to review his manuscript and to write the foreword of his book.

We were in the same class at Yale. I studied Molecular Biophysics and Biochemistry and even so I began a surprisingly deep love affair with cuisine and wine which redirected me ultimately away from academia and on to becoming a professional chef and restaurateur.

The hamburger has been a recurring item of contemplation throughout my career and it gives me delight to report that this book is both scrupulously researched and written with graceful style. I could not put it down and finished in a single sitting. Ever so hungry before I reached the end.

Not unsurprisingly, the bittersweet disillusionment of the faux New Haven hamburger legend is eclipsed by the author's quest for the truth.

As a result, we find ourselves in a deeper community – one created by unity achieved in pursuit of light and truth. *Lux et veritas*.

Craig Shelton
James Beard Award-Winning Chef
Shelton Hospitality Group
Bedminster, New Jersey

ACKNOWLEDGEMENTS

Since this effort was akin to solving a criminal case, I brought Sir Arthur Conan Doyle's magnificent detective Sherlock Holmes to act as my muse in this venture. In that moment, I morphed from mild-mannered newspaper columnist to (add booming voice) The Hamburger Detective!

As with any detective, the case begins with discovery. This was a very cold case. The trail had long been covered by the ravages of time, misinformation, and, well, disinformation. Luckily, my son Peter, in the tradition of his grandfather, has adopted his own certain set of investigative skills in the area of genealogy. With the help of such tools like Social Security records, Ancestry.com, and newspapers.com, he's been able to recreate our family tree. One evening, he casually said, "Dad, why don't you use these for your research." Viola! All of the sudden the discovery of evidence gushed forth.

But I knew others had followed this scent before me, and I didn't want to repeat their research if I didn't have to. With the help of Dave Lieber of the *Dallas Morning News* I was able to obtain original source material on the roots of the Fletcher Davis story. This allowed me to add some color to the work already done by the late Josh Ozersky. Similarly, Pam Vaccaro's work proved extremely relevant.

I didn't rely on personal interviews to make the case presented in *Hamburger Dreams*. (Detectives from Sherlock Holmes to Columbo demonstrate the need to find support to supplement eye-witness testimony.) Still, the story behind the story was recent enough (1985) for primary witnesses to still be alive. To the extent possible, I sought to interview them. John Menches provided tremendous help with introducing me to members of his extended family, including Judy Kusmits and Ron Bush.

Jim Baker, historian for the Town of Hamburg provided important original documents. He also put me in touch with Jack Edson and

Esther Kowal, a librarian at the Frontier Central School District. Marty Biniasz graciously opened the historical archives to the Erie County Agricultural Society.

Speaking of school, I must acknowledge the vast help of my classmates in the Yale Class of 1982. Bird served as my research associate during a foray through Buffalo. A somewhat facetious "what I did over the summer" post to our class Facebook group generated inordinate interest. Perhaps it was because they all recalled buying a hamburger at Louis' Lunch. John Tomko, Robin Lyn, and Julie Hanselmann all pointed me to excellent reviewers and Craig Shelton (a James Beard Award-winning chef) even agreed to write the foreword.

Columnists friends helped, too. Pam Sherman introduced me to Dr. Beth Forrest of the Culinary Institute of America for a review.

This book would never have been completed without the motivation and help of Betsy, my wonderful wife. She put up with me as I scoured arcane alleys of history (and real-life). She had the smarts to convince me to contact her classmate Martha Foster and her husband David, proprietors of a McDonald's in Bath, New York. Martha was kind enough to help me find the right person to speak to about McDonald's role in this story (and, as you'll see, it was quite critical).

As usual, Betsy tirelessly proofed the manuscript and found my many mistakes. Again, as usual, I made changes subsequent to her corrections that may have slipped through the editing process. Those are on me, not her. Finally, I want to thank my daughters, Catarina (for helping me with the cover and the footnotes – which are more important in *Hamburger Dreams* since I want future researchers to know exactly where to look as they continue to explore this story) and Cesidia (who helped during the promotion of the book).

Christopher Carosa
Mendon, New York
November 30, 2018

PROLOGUE:
THE GREATEST CULINARY MYSTERY IN HISTORY

APRIL 29, 1982. NEW HAVEN, CONNECTICUT. It was the final days of my final term of my final year in college. Four years of hard work would soon reward me with a Bachelor of Science (Intensive) Degree in Physics and Astronomy. My senior project completed, I had one final paper due on this day. It was a term paper for a course called "Study of the City." I was more anxious about the men's softball finals that afternoon than the paper. I was supposed to be the starting pitcher. (It turned out I wasn't, but that's a tale for another time.)

I had no interest in urban planning. That was my brother's bailiwick. The course "Study of the City" came recommended by several classmates, who also took it. They made a big deal about the instructor Alexander Garvin. They spoke as if I should have recognized his name. I didn't.

Garvin, it turned out, was more than merely another Yale graduate returning to his alma mater to bequeath his vast knowledge and experience to the next generation. Unlike most (but not all) of the professors whose classes I sat in, Garvin had real world experience. He served as the deputy commissioner of the New York City's Housing & Development Administration department. In short, he was a big deal. Or at least that's what my architecture major classmates told me. I had no reason to disagree with them.

But I had my doubts about attending the class. I remember casually mentioning this to my brother Kenny, then a junior at the University of Buffalo. He was majoring in Environmental Design. When I told him of this class "Study of the City" and the background of the instructor, he had but one request: "Can I take the class instead of you?" Needless to say, given my brother's ardent enthusiasm for the subject, I had no choice but to enroll.

What excited him most about "Study of the City," however, was the term paper required to complete the course. Garvin had us write the "biography" of our home town. In my case, this would be Buffalo, New York. My brother immediately volunteered to secure source documents for me. He did. He sent me original material he had used for his papers. He contacted the Buffalo Chamber of Commerce and had them forward me all the relevant materials they had.

Of course, I needed more. Fortunately, Yale had (and continues to have) a very big library (Sterling Memorial Library, second largest in the world). In one of my infrequent trips to its stacks, I took out several books and one very old (from 1888) newspaper. Of those, only the newspaper made it into my term paper's bibliography. I still have that term paper. That's why I can remember the newspaper. I don't remember what those other books were, though.

What I do remember is this.

In the course of my research, I discovered an interesting tidbit from one of the source materials I borrowed from Sterling Library. Apparently, the hamburger had been invented at the Erie County Fair in the mid-1880's. I told this to my classmates. One of them, a native of New Haven, instantly rejected the claim. He confidently insisted the real birthplace of the hamburger was Louis' Lunch, just a few blocks away from where we sat in downtown New Haven.

The next day he took me there for lunch. I was grateful, but not impressed. I could tell by the look on his face he thought it was the greatest thing since sliced bread. Ironically, the sandwich was served on sliced bread.

I returned the reading materials I had taken out of the library never to see them again. Like I said, I don't remember the books, but I do remember getting scolded by the librarian. She took one look at the 1888 newspaper and accused me of trying to steal it. That was an odd charge since I was returning it. When I asked her to explain herself, she said, "That belongs in the rare books library."

Years later, when writing *50 Hidden Gems of Greater Western New York*, (Pandamensional Solutions, 2012), I wanted to include a chapter about the origin of the hamburger. I went back to Yale. This time to the Beinecke Rare Book & Manuscript Library. I found a very interested research librarian who happened to be from Western New York. We looked up the reference to the newspaper in the card catalog. Alas, when we went to shelf where it should have been located, there was an empty space. Upon further investigation, the research librarian discovered the newspaper had been "purged" a few years earlier.

Who knew they purged "rare" books? Kinda defeats the purpose, if you ask me.

Nonetheless, I thought I had a smoking gun. Instead, I was left with a mystery – the greatest culinary mystery in history.

I promised myself, when I had the time, I would try my best to solve this mystery.

That time has now come...

ACT ONE:

– MATERIAL EVIDENCE –

THE SCENE, THE SUSPECTS, AND THE MOTIVATION

CHAPTER ONE:
THE QUESTION THAT CHANGED HISTORY

Hiram P. Hopkins woke up Friday morning to threatening skies.[1] The skies didn't bother him. After the last nine months, nothing more could bother him. It was the last day of the annual Erie County Fair. He had accomplished much, despite his apparent youth. Why should that have surprised anyone?

He inhaled a deep satisfying breath of the moist morning air. For a moment, Hiram's mind drifted back to another morning nine months earlier. *"The Erie County Agricultural Society held its annual meeting at Kopp's Hotel, Abbott's Corners, Wednesday, Jan. 21st. H.P. Hopkins of Buffalo was elected president."* He remembered reading that in *The Buffalo Commercial* the previous January. He was but twenty-nine years old when the Society tapped him to replace long-time president John Kraus.

For the son of former State Comptroller Nelson K. Hopkins, this came as a natural ascendency. He was only fourteen when he presented a portrait of Governor De Witt Clinton as a gift to the City of Buffalo's then new Grosvenor Library. At age sixteen, New York State Governor John Adams Dix appointed Hiram Aide-de-Camp, assigning him the rank of colonel. He travelled across New York State as a part of the governor's military staff. Again, he was only sixteen.

Now a land owner, a respected dairy farmer, and a winner of several major premiums at previous fairs, Hiram felt comfortable with both over-achieving and traveling in higher circles. A well-regarded equestrian, when he wasn't busy raising his prize-winning dairy cows – "the finest herd of Jersey Cattle" in Western New York according to one newspaper account – Hiram played polo and joined fox hunting excursions as far away as the Genesee River Valley.

Still, some might have thought Hiram too young to take on the task of running one of New York State's largest county fairs. Indeed, those first few months following his election challenged the now thirty-year-old scion of two of Buffalo's most prominent families. While successful, the previous year's Erie County Fair had exposed some room for improvement. The ladies department desired more attention. The new grandstand needed finishing. Overall, a feeling pervaded that enhancements were required to put the fairgrounds in Hamburg in "first-class order."

Beyond the local sentiments, the politics of the county fair business confronted Hiram as soon as he proudly announced the dates of the 1885 Erie County Fair. In April, the board of directors approved the traditional week in late September. Along with the September 22-25 dates came a detailed schedule of all the premium races on each day of the Fair.

Within a few days, however, newspapers began reporting that the New York State Breeders' Association had selected those same dates for their Western New York Fair at Rochester. In the ensuing stare down, Hiram and the Erie County Agricultural Society blinked first. At their May meeting, the directors consented. The Erie County Fair was to be moved to September 15-18.

In June, with only short three months to go, Hiram and the Society finally got down to business. They conceded to the ladies department and approved building the new Domestic Hall with a unique octagon design. But this effort to appease also led to some confusion. It was first reported the building would be designed and built by Hamburg Planing Mill Company, the same company that built the new grandstand a year earlier. In the end, however, the contract was awarded to Hoffmeyer and Getz of Buffalo.

The next controversy came in August, when the Board voted to do away with the old "Family ticket system." In its place, they adopted a new pricing scale for tickets. People complained. Two weeks before the Fair, the Board reversed its decision and returned to the old way of issuing one-price Family Tickets.

The bad news continued. Entries were down for both the pigs category and the ladies department. Worse, the ladies department Domestic Hall still wasn't done. Would this be a repeat of last year when the new grandstand debuted in not-quite-finished condition? Heading into the 1885 Fair, who could blame Hiram if he was a tad bit anxious.

But, on this day – September 18, 1885 – all that was behind him. It was the final day of the Erie County Fair. By most accounts, after the previous day's record-breaking attendance, it would soon be considered the best yet. Nothing could depress Hiram's budding euphoria.

Not even the impending rain.

After all, he won his first prize at the 1878 Erie County Fair, a fair postponed by a "persistent three-day rainstorm." Far from ominous, Hiram saw the rain as a good omen.

Walking the fairgrounds under darkening skies before the gates opened that Friday morning, Hiram surveyed the vast expanse of his accomplishment. All around the grounds he saw happy faces beneath the many vendor tents and booths that dotted the landscape. As a result of Thursday's dense crowds, they were no doubt flush with cash. If they were worried about the chance of rain, they didn't show it.

As Hiram neared the now-finished grandstand, he did spy upon two dour faces. These were the Ohio brothers. A few years younger than he was, Hiram took a natural liking to them. He wandered over to their tent to see what troubled them.

"Mr. Hopkins," began the older brother, "we've sold out of sausage for our sandwiches. Do you know where we could buy more?"

Hiram reflected for a moment. He felt a raindrop touch him. He knew exactly who the boys should go to.

It may have seemed inconsequential at the time, but, in that instant, Hiram P. Hopkins' answer would forever change mankind in a way that continues to touch nearly every man, woman, and child in the world today…

CHAPTER TWO:
MANKIND'S (SECOND) GREATEST INVENTION

"I'll gladly pay you Tuesday for a hamburger today."

When J. Wellington Wimpy first voiced that phrase on December 28, 1934 in Fleischer Studios short "We Aim to Please," Popeye's 17th theatrical cartoon,[1] the White Castle hamburger chain had already been around for 13 years.[2] Indeed, by the time E.C. Segar added the character of Wimpy to his King Features Syndicate cartoon *Thimble Theatre* in 1931,[3] White Castle was well on its way to selling 50 million hamburgers. It would achieve that mark in 1941.[4]

A year earlier, brothers Dick and Mac McDonald moved their father's food stand from Route 66 in Monrovia, California to the streets of San Bernardino. They rechristened their restaurant "McDonald's Bar-B-Que."[5] Eight years later they converted their carhops to self-serve and reduced the menu to burgers, fries, and milkshakes. They reopened their new fast food establishment on December 12, 1948 under the name "McDonald's."[6]

That same year Harry and Esther Snyder opened the first In-N-Out Burger in Baldwin Park, California just outside of Los Angeles. It would be the first fast food restaurant in the state of California to feature a drive-thru ordering and pick-up system.[7] By 1958, on their ten-year anniversary, In-N-Out's five locations celebrated by switching from bottled pop to fountain drinks.[8] (In contrast, Wisconsin's Sheboygan County celebrated the opening of McDonald's 121st restaurant on June 19, 1958.)[9]

A year later, in 1959, two Miami franchisees (and Cornell grads) – James McLamore and David Edgerton – bought the faltering Insta-Burger King company.[10] The duo immediately renamed it "Burger King" and expanded it to 250 restaurants by the time they sold the business to Pillsbury in 1967.[11] (In contrast, McDonald's opened its 1,000th restaurant in 1968 in Des Plaines, Illinois.)[12]

The very next year, on November 15, 1969, Dave Thomas, after becoming a millionaire working for Colonel Harland Sanders,[13] opened the first Wendy's in Columbus, Ohio.[14] Today, Wendy's sports more than 6,000 locations.[15] (In contrast, McDonald's has more than 36,000 restaurants in operation today.)[16]

Although the fast food business began in earnest at the outset of the roaring twenties,[17] it took the logistical problem solvers of World War II, as well as America's growing love affair with the automobile, to provide both the business model and the systems technology to get the industry as we know it today off the ground. Just how big is this industry? In the United States alone, fast food generated $200 billion in revenue during the year 2015.[18] Worldwide revenues topped $570 billion.[19]

Nearly every one of us has either worked at a fast food restaurant or knows someone who has. Today, the trade employs approximately four million people.[20] While encompassing many types of food, it's clear there is one item that spurred this industry: the hamburger. This makes the hamburger possibly the second most important invention in all of mankind's history.[21]

Thanks in part to both government statistics and required disclosures of publicly traded companies, when it comes to the burger business, we possess a veritable cornucopia of data, information, and history over the past 100 years or so. Yet, the actual origins of the hamburger sandwich remain hidden in the cloudy realm of hearsay, hype, and hometown hope. Close your eyes for a moment and let's explore the leading suspects behind these mysterious tales of the birth of the first hamburger…

CHAPTER THREE:
THOSE AMAZING MENCHES BOYS

Brothers Charles and Frank Menches were prolific concessionaires. They didn't start that way. By the time he was twenty, Charles had a "successful season" with the Bob Stickney circus. Contemporary reporters called him a "thoroughly proficient" trapeze artist.[1] After spending several years as a high wire and trapeze artist with both the Stickney circus and the Old John Robinson circus, Charles decided to enter the concession business full-time with his brother Frank in 1884.[2]

Frank, six years younger than Charles, was no slouch when it came to athleticism, either. He was an award-winning bicycle racer, competing into his early twenties.[3,4]

Born in Canton, Ohio to Franco-Prussian immigrants, the brothers dove into multiple business ventures at an early age. While working with the circus, Charles began dabbling in concession sales. Very quickly, he determined selling food and drink brought in more profits – and was considerably safer – than performing death-defying gymnastics several stories in the air. That led to his decision to leave Stickney. Still, the circus proved a useful experience. It gave him and his brother both credibility (remember, in 1884 Frank was only nineteen and Charles was twenty-five) and, more critically, connections.[5]

Charles remained captivated by the showmanship of performing. When the Menches Brothers were awarded the drink and food concession at the Summit County Fair, Charles couldn't hold back. In a 1938 interview, Frank recalled, "We erected a couple of telegraph poles inside the track, opposite the grand stand. We strung a high wire from the top of the grand stand to one of the poles – and Charles walked it. We gave an exhibition of wire walking and trapeze acts. Charles was the star in that line – although I did some work on the rings."[6]

Throughout this period, the brothers operated a cigar store on Tuscarawas Street in their home town. It's likely to have been a burden to be on the road and run a retail store. Indeed, when the store was robbed in 1884, an eyewitness didn't run to see either of the brothers. He ran to report the suspicious activity to their parents.[7] The brothers also owned a grocery store a few doors down on Tuscarawas Street.[8]

Remember those connections referred to earlier? They didn't just arise from Charles' circus career. Their cigar store was located in close proximity to the law offices of William McKinley.[9] At the time, McKinley was serving in Congress, but by 1892 he would become governor of the State of Ohio and, in 1896, President of the United States.

The Menches brothers had more than a passing acquaintance with the future president. Charles briefly (1887) partnered in business (the Menches & Barber Circus, of course) with Orrin Barber, the nephew of McKinley's wife.[10] Despite the eventual falling out with Barber,[11] the brothers remained close with McKinley. How do we know this? Because in December of 1891, McKinley wrote a glowing letter on behalf of these "deserving young men" to one of the directors of the upcoming Chicago World's Fair advocating the Menches Brothers be awarded the popcorn concession for the event.[12]

By the time McKinley wrote his letter of recommendation, the brothers' concession business had taken off. In 1889 the Stark County Fair (Canton, Ohio) awarded them major concession rights to "dispense lunch and eatables from two stands near the Grand Stand."[13] In 1891, the Summit County Fair (Akron, Ohio) granted Frank and Charles exclusive food and soft drink concession rights. The brothers retained these rights until the 1913 flood ended that fair.[14]

Charles and Frank Menches were successful entrepreneurs, entertainers, and inventors. While they may have been entertainers in their heart, they "made their nut" (to borrow a phrase John C. Kunzog attributed to Frank[15]) via the concessions business rather than through performance. "Charles quickly discovered he could make more money selling popcorn, candy, and peanuts than he could as a trapeze artist," says John Menches, the great grandson of Charles Menches.[16]

The Menches brothers began their concession business at just the right time. Shortly after the Civil War, the United States was hit with several boom and bust economic cycles. One of the worst was the Depression of 1882-1885. During the infamous Panic of 1884, 5% of all American factories and mines were completely shut down and another 5% were partially closed, leaving nearly 1 million people out of work.[17] By focusing on country fairs and races, the Menches brothers avoided the heavily industrialized urban areas. This insulated them from the frequent late-nineteenth century recessions.

Their concession business soon grew beyond fair, expositions, and tracks. Seeing opportunity in the next town over, Frank and Charles relocated from their hometown of Canton, Ohio to nearby Akron in 1897.[18] In 1899 the Menches Brothers became proprietors of Summit Lake Park.[19] This resort and entertainment venue included acrobats, singers, dancers, and even a theater. Again, no doubt their old circus connections came in handy. In 1901, they bought adjacent property that included baseball fields and started hosting baseball games.[20]

By 1902, they seemed "to have a monopoly on the candy, peanut and popcorn business" at the Summit County Fair.[21] With the concession business thriving at both the park and the county fairs, the Menches brothers created a confectionary manufacturer to supply their various ventures. Called "Premium Candy and Corn," the Menches brothers experimented to create novelty products. They called one of those "Gee-Whiz" popcorn – essentially caramel popcorn and peanuts. Sound familiar? Today we call it "Crackerjacks" (although the Crackerjacks company does not refer to the Menches Brothers in their own origin story).[22]

Things didn't go so well at Summit Lake Park when the Northern Ohio Traction Company realigned their routes. Summit Lake Park found itself outside that realignment and the Menches Brothers declared bankruptcy in 1903.[23] They came out of bankruptcy in 1904,[24] just in time for the Louisiana Purchase Exposition. This event is more commonly known as the 1904 St. Louis World's Fair. It was there that Charles is said to have discovered the idea of wrapping a waffle into a conical shape to create a cone to place ice cream in. The family believes it was Frank who came up with the idea of creating the cone using a "fid," a wooden tool shaped like a cylinder to unravel rope.[25]

Whatever the origin, the idea was a hit. Selling ice cream cones at their booths, the Menches Brothers couldn't keep up with demand. They retrofitted their Premium Candy and Corn company to produce ice cream cones and changed its name to "Premium Candy, Corn and Cone Company."[26] They couldn't get a patent on the ice cream cone itself, so Charles got a patent on the next best thing – the waffle iron used to make the cones.[27] At its height, the company made 60,000 cones a day.[28] All the while, they maintained their concessionaire business, selling sausage, hamburgers, oysters, drinks, cigars, and, of course, ice cream cones.

The boys built their homes with the profits from this enterprise. But nothing lasts forever. By 1916, the Menches brothers couldn't match their competitors who had better capital. They sold Premium Candy, Corn and Cone Company. With the proceeds from the sale, they built the Liberty Theater just as the motion picture business started to explode.[29] Once again, they hopped on a wave just as it was beginning to crest. They also built a hotel, restaurant and a novelty balloon company because, well, you can't say "Menches" without also saying "novelty."[30]

They continued to operate concession stands at local county fairs into the 1920s, but focused most of their energies on the Liberty Theater. When Charles died in 1931, his obituary played up his role in the invention of the ice cream cone and mentioned his part in inventing the hamburger as an aside.[31] When Frank died in 1951, his obituary played up his role in the invention of the hamburger and mentioned his part in inventing the ice cream cone as an aside.[32]

Their real legacy, though, appeared in the closing paragraph of a story that ran in 1932. It reads, "[the] Menches [brothers] will not be commemorated by an expensive monument and [their] name may never reach the pages of the encyclopedias, but [they] did [their] bit in making people happier."[33]

Did the Menches Brothers serve the first hamburger in 1885 at the Erie County Fair in Hamburg, New York? They have the honor of owning the first recorded hamburger origin story. As we shall see in a later chapter, it's complicated.

Unlike the Menches brothers, our remaining suspects unfortunately don't have the same degree of documented legacy. Still, the historical record does provide a reasonable hint to their lives and their motivations. We explore their life stories in the next three chapters.

CHAPTER FOUR:
CHARLES "HAMBURGER CHARLIE" NAGREEN

The race was over. The rush was about to begin.

Clad in a now dirty white apron and a matching white vendor hat coming to a point above his head, Emil Wurm leaned out over the counter beneath the tent-like awning. His hands steadied him as he tried to maintain balance on his outstretched tippy-toes. The roar of the thousands in the grandstand meant the show was over. Soon, all of the morning's hard work would reap its reward.

His teenage eyes wide with anticipation, Emil peered at the gates of the track, waiting for the first sign of the impending torrent of hungry customers. Behind him seven other workers readied themselves for the expected onslaught. At the grill stood Charles Nagreen, owner of the stand, "Hamburger Charlie" himself. In a few moments, fairgoers would come delight in one of the many items Charlie dished up in his stand. In the typical rush after the show, it wouldn't be unusual for the stand to sell 150 pounds of hamburgers and 75 pounds of hot dogs.[1]

To tell the story of how Charles Nagreen became Hamburger Charlie, we need to go back more than a half century earlier. To a time when a territory would become a state…

During the mid-nineteenth century, the sparse population in the small towns and hamlets north of Oshkosh, Wisconsin no doubt knew each other well. And everybody knew Uncle Andrew. Wisconsin Territory applied for statehood in 1848 and became the 30th state in the United States on May 29th of that same year. By the 1850 census, the new state's population exceeded 300,000, with more than a third coming from Western New York and New England.[2] Others would soon come. Among those included Andrew and Adelia Rhoades.

The Rhoades, originally of Onondaga, New York, first moved to Ohio in 1836 before settling in Medina, Wisconsin in 1854. Once there, Andrew built the Rhoades House, a hotel noted for its "home-like hospitality."[3] The Rhoades House found itself in the prime location on the main road from the lumber woods near Seymour and Shawano and the sawmill town of Appleton. It quickly earned a reputation as "a famous place of entertainment, popular all over the region."[4]

"Uncle" Andrew and "Aunt" Delia hosted many parties and dances for their guests. Their hostelry had a hall on the second floor designed specifically for this purpose. Andrew was called "the fiddler" and provided the only music for the occasion. He often regaled dancers with his favorite tune, "The Old Irish Washerwoman."[5]

Whether it was a "grand dance for New Year's Eve,[6] an "old-fashioned ball" on the Fourth of July,[7] or simply a masquerade dance to combat those winter blahs in the middle of February,[8] Uncle Andrew was more than pleased to throw a rollicking good time.

It's only fitting then, that a jolly fellow like Andrew Rhoades would be the "victim" of not one but two false death notices. His first obituary appeared in 1896, where it was reported that he died in his home from pneumonia.[9] A week later, a competing newspaper wrote "Word comes from Medina today that Mr. Rhoades is very ill but is not dead."[10]

The second story surfaced five years later in 1901. This one said he died rich and willed everything to his destitute sister.[11] Again, a competing newspaper exposed the fake news. Apparently, not only was Uncle Andrew very much alive, but he was very much not rich. He did, though, have a sister "in reduced circumstances" who he invited to live in his hotel.[12]

When death finally came knocking, Uncle Andrew proved more resilient than doctors expected. In July 1904, as Charles Menches was said to be discovering the ice cream cone, Andrew Rhoades suffered a second stroke a mere five weeks after the first. Doctors said "a third and fatal stroke may come any moment."[13] Less than two months after this dire prediction, however, it was reported "Mr. Andrew Rhoades has been feeling some better for the past week."[14] In fact, by the following March, though the stroke "seriously affected his speech,"[15] Uncle Andrew "was enough better so he was able to sit up and play his old violin."[16] He died four months later in July, 1905, just two months shy of his ninetieth birthday.[17]

Compare the happy-go-lucky life of Andrew Rhoades to the dour life of Joseph Nagreen. Born in 1824 in Austria, he emigrated to America in the 1850's, quickly marrying and moving his young family from Illinois to Hortonville, Wisconsin in 1866. A cabinet-making and undertaker,[18] Joseph might seem a bit glum next to Uncle Andrew. There was a good reason for that.

Joseph Nagreen arrived in New York in 1852 a grizzled twenty-seven-year-old veteran. By the time he came to America, he had already served in the Austrian army for eight years. He fought foreign wars as a member of the Prince Carl Infantry. He didn't leave his homeland to escape military service. In fact, Joseph joined (and re-enlisted in when his first tour expired) F Company of the 13th Illinois infantry, serving for three years on the Union side of America's Civil War. He saw action across the south from Lime Creek, Missouri to the Siege of Vicksburg in Mississippi.[19]

In his eleven years of active military service, Nagreen never suffered a serious injury. The battle of Chickasaw Bayou, Mississippi in late December 1862, however, almost killed him. During the heat of the fight, Nagreen found safety behind a large tree stump. His heart racing as he collected himself, his world suddenly exploded – literally.

The stump took a direct hit from a Confederate cannon ball. Momentarily stunned, when he recovered his senses Joseph was surprised to discover he could walk. More important: he could run. A squad of Mississippi cavalrymen quickly converged on him. Union soldiers rained a volley of bullets on the entire ensemble. Nagreen's veteran instincts told him to play possum among the lifeless bodies around him. He remained inert until the guns stopped firing. Ultimately, it wasn't bullets that ended Nagreen's military career – it was sunstroke, from which he received an honorable discharge in 1864.[20]

Joseph Nagreen led a hard life. Four of his eleven children died young. He was forced to quit his furniture business in 1884 due to poor health (which couldn't have been too poor because he lived another three decades, surviving on his Civil War pension). A year later, his third youngest son, Charles, decided to find a way to earn money. Though he was fifteen at the time, Charles R. Nagreen sought a career path different from his older brother Orlando. Orlando Nagreen, eight years older than Charles, began working as a farm laborer at the age of twelve before leaving to work in the mines east of Ironwood.[21]

It was time for Charles to make a decision. On the one hand, there was his now visually impaired father's quiet life of cabinetry. On the other hand, there was the ever-popular Uncle Andrew. In a way, Charles combined the best of both worlds. He gathered the requisite raw materials and built a food stand at the various county fairs throughout the region.[22] By 1890, following directly in the footsteps of Andrew Rhoades, Charles Nagreen was listed as the manager of the St. Patrick's dance at the town hall in nearby Shiocton, Wisconsin.[23] By 1917 he was billed as "Hamburger Charlie" (or "Hamburger Charley," depending on the newspaper) serving refreshments at various picnics, pleasure excursions, and dances.[24,25,26,27]

During the off season, Hamburger Charlie reverted to his "Charles Nagreen" alter-ego. Despite the change in persona, the naturally outgoing Nagreen remained a salesman. His daughter Violet once remarked "he would sell fireworks, costumes, and even Christmas trees. He also owned an ice cream shop."[28]

In Charles Nagreen, it would seem while you can take the barker out of the carnival, you can't take the carnival out of the barker. Charlie would often take his ice cream out of the store and bring it directly to populated neighborhoods – an early version of "the ice cream man" generations of young children look forward to every summer. Only instead of using a motorized truck, he used a horse-drawn wagon. And, according to Violet, he trained that horse to stop as soon as it saw an eager customer running towards the wagon.[29] Charlie well understood the art of sales.

To win the sale, Charlie knew you had to first attract the customer. How did he do this? He took a lesson right from Uncle Andrews' playbook. "When business was slow, Charlie would get out his guitar and mouth organ and play a few tunes," said Emil Wurm, who began working at Charlie's Dew Drop Inn ice cream parlor at the age of 12 in 1917 and then traveled with his boss on the annual summer fair circuit until 1923. Wurm recalls, "He sang old favorites and that usually would draw a crowd. Part of his purpose was entertainment, but once he drew a crowd he would start marketing his burgers. He would chant something like, 'Hey you skinny rascals don't you ever eat?' or 'We have seats to sit down and rest your poor old grandmother.'"[30]

For Nagreen – "Hamburger Charlie" – it was the summer season that defined his true purpose in life. He lived for the fair. Indeed, he would continue manning his little lunch stand through the decades until his death in 1951 (just months before Frank Menches died) finally prevented him from flipping one last burger.

Did Hamburger Charlie serve the first hamburger at the Seymour Fair the same year as the Menches Brothers? The Menches Brothers and Charles Nagreen might be considered "the usual suspects" in our culinary WhoDunIt. Our next suspect comes from a very different background – and a very different part of the country.

CHAPTER FIVE:
LOUIS LASSEN AND LOUIS' LUNCH

W hat do you do with 6,000 surplus U.S. Army war wagons? That's precisely the predicament the government found itself in at the close of the Civil War. Most found their way from storage at the Quartermaster Depot in Washington D.C to Fort Leavenworth, Kansas, where they would be pressed into service for use by military outposts on the Great Plains and beyond.[1]

The close of the Civil War ushered in the advent of the classic cattle drive. You might think this is relevant because a single half-ton steer produces 1,000 hamburgers[2], but there's a more interesting reason to reference these quintessential western events.

Lacking an adequate railroad network, for two decades cowboys would lead cattle on often dangerous trails from ranch head to slaughter house. In 1866, Charles Goodnight and Oliver Loving decided to blaze a new trail from Fort Belknap, Texas to Fort Sumner, New Mexico.[3] Goodnight realized he needed a good supply of food for his hired hands. He bought one of those surplus Civil War wagons and refashioned it.[4] He packed food and cooking utensils into a chuck box which featured a lid that, when opened, provided the cook with a flat surface to prepare the food.[5] Goodnight called it a "Grub Wagon," but we know it today by the name "Chuckwagon" (named after the box, not its inventor).[6]

What? You say you've never heard of Charles Goodnight? Maybe not, but you certainly know of him, if only by another name. Said to have been "established in the rank of mythical heroes" among the true icons of the west,[7] several of Goodnight's famous adventures have been chronicled in fictional stories of that era. Most famously, John Wayne portrayed his real-life rescue of a girl captured by Comanches (as Ethan Edwards in John Ford's 1956 epic *The Searchers*). More recently, we saw Goodnight through the character Woodrow F. Call in Larry McMurtry's

1985 epic novel *Lonesome Dove* (and as portrayed by Tommy Lee Jones in the 1989 television miniseries of the same name).

Incidentally, two years after Goodnight invented the Chuckwagon, George Pullman unveiled a more sophisticated "meals on wheels" concept. In the spring of 1868, he invited several dozen dignitaries and journalists to take a ride in the "Delmonico," the first true railroad dining car.[8] Note the name "Delmonico." It appears again in a later chapter. And so will the railroad dining car, only sooner. But, first, let's give Charles Goodnight credit for the novel invention of his "Grub Wagon," for its evolution plays an important role in our story.

Once started, the utility of "a moveable feast" became evident to all. While railroad dining cars weren't quite adaptable to other uses (yet), within a decade of Goodnight's first use, Chuckwagons found their way onto farms during harvest time.[9] Bringing them out into the vast fields allowed farmhands to work virtually uninterrupted for the entire day. All they would need was a single short break for lunch, courtesy of Goodnight's invention.

As the expanded rail network reduced the necessity for cattle drives and their attendant chuckwagons in the west, a version of the chuckwagon – the lunch wagon – began to appear in the east. Initially at country fairs,[10] lunch wagons became a mainstay in urban areas, especially among nightshift workers.[11] These portable food carts became especially popular, particularly in New England. By 1894, while Hartford, Connecticut had but one, Worcester, Massachusetts, home of the first lunch wagon, had nineteen; Providence, Rhode Island had seventeen; Springfield, Massachusetts had nine; and, Boston, the granddaddy of them all, had seventy-two.[12]

A year (or maybe three) later, a new lunch wagon opened in New Haven, Connecticut.

Although several sources claim Louis Lassen emigrated from Germany or Denmark to New Haven in 1886 when he was 21 years old,[13,14] an 1885 New Haven newspaper article refers to a "Mr. Louis Lassen" as a member of the German Baptist Sunday school committee.[15] A year later he sang in a quartet at the Christmas festival of the Sunday school.[16] Lassen remained involved in the German Baptist church through at least 1901.[17] He also participated with other German voters in New Haven in support of the Republican party,[18] eventually serving as vice president for the Republican committee.[19]

In 1886, the daily newspaper mentioned a "Lewis Lassen" as paying $24 (the equivalent of $645 in 2018) for a retail license to comply with the then new Oleomargarine Law.[20] This controversial law, promoted by the dairy industry, "placed a heavy license tax on manufacturers, wholesalers, and retailers."[21] "Lewis" is likely a misspelling of Lassen's first name as sources indicate he became a food peddler selling butter and eggs shortly after immigrating to America[22]. Roughly a decade later, Lassen's "food cart" became a full-fledged lunch wagon.

The year may have been 1897, as early advertising stated.[23] Indeed, initially at least, the successor restaurant itself proclaimed on its sign: "Louis Lunch – Est. 1897".[24] Alternatively, and as generally accepted today, Lassen may have started serving lunch in 1895. This date change seems to have occurred no later than 1967,[25] likely as a result of more intense research as to the exact origins of Louis' Lunch. We'll see what prompted this research in Chapter 8. (Incidentally, both reporters and the family itself refer to the eatery as "Louis Lunch" and "Louis' Lunch," leaving one to wonder as to the actual intent regarding the apostrophe. To make it easier for readers in this book, we've chosen to include the apostrophe unless citing original source material where the apostrophe is omitted, including the restaurant's sign itself.)

Louis' "lunch" wagon began offering lunch items to factory workers on Meadow Street by the New Haven train station and traveled between two factories located on Temple and George Street.[26] Business thrived as customers flocked to the lunch wagon for Louis' tasty "'Egg Trilby' (one egg over light with a thin slice of onion).[27] In 1907, Lassen decided to make his eatery less mobile and bought an old railroad dining car to replace his lunch wagon.[28,29] (See, I told you the railroad diner would reappear in this story.) He selected a site by a pre-Civil War tannery on the corner of George and Temple Streets.[30] At that time, a harness shop occupied the tannery's small office building in front.[31]

In 1916, Louis, along with his son Ervin who was now helping him, ditched the diner car and moved into the small 12-foot by 18-foot office building.[32] Father and son immediately began to redesign the interior to mimic what they though an English pub looked like. Within that cramped, one-room space they fashioned a kitchenette area with two small iron stoves. The floor of the kitchen featured a trap door from which one would descend by ladder into a basement. They'd prepare each days' food in this cellar. A thick timber slab counter separated the cooking area from the dining area where "a heavy wooden bench along one wall, a few booths tucked into the corners, and the well-engraved counter with three stools provide only 14 seats."[33]

Louis brought all his family into the business. His grandson Ken recalled, "I used to help my grandfather grind the meat, even before I went to kindergarten. A good part of my heart and soul are in this place. I've worked here since the 1920's when my father and his brothers ran it."[34,35] Ken wanted to be an architect, but when his father Ervin died in 1946, he inherited the restaurant.[36]

Did Louis Lassen serve the first hamburger from his lunch wagon in 1900? He may have, but it was through Ken's initiative that we have come to understand the rich legacy of Louis' Lunch. In a moment, we'll delve deeper into this story – which itself could comprise a separate book – but first we need to take a peek at our two final suspects. Are they really two or are they the same? The next two chapters will give you an important clue.

CHAPTER SIX:
1904 ST. LOUIS WORLD'S FAIR

*P*anem et Circenses. It's a philosophy that goes back to ancient Rome. Literally translated from the original Latin as "Breads and Circuses," it defines a strategy to mollify a potentially unruly populace by distracting them with basic needs and entertainment. It's what you do if you're not sure the sudden surge in pitchfork sales are destined for farms across your nation or a dense mob about to knock down your front door.

Such was the condition of France throughout the period of the French Revolution. The new government, recognizing its tenuous position, organized a series of festivities beginning with the Festival of the Federation held on July 14, 1790, a year to the day after that aforementioned mob stormed the Bastille. During the final stages of *Révolution française*, and well after the Reign of Terror, the Directory ruled France. In 1798, a little more than a year before the *coup d'état* that ushered in a new triumvirate that included Napoleon Bonaparte, the Directory decided to sponsor an industrial exposition.

The French First Republic's exposition ran from September 19, 1798 through October 1, 1798. Though modest, the country continued to host these expositions through the Napoleonic Era, the Bourbon Restoration, the July Monarchy, until the Second Republic sponsored the eleventh and final exposition in 1849. By that time, other major European cities offered similar fairs. It was decided, rather than hold competing events, a singular show composed of all the European nations should be held.

Many consider the Great Exhibition of the Works of Industry of All Nations ("The Great Exhibition") to be the very first "World's Fair." Held in London from May 1, 1851 through October 15, 1851, it was co-hosted by Prince Albert, Queen Victoria's husband. It also featured a huge building built especially for the exposition. Called "The Crystal

Palace," this expansive (1,848 feet by 454 feet) structure was composed of glass and iron. Still, it managed to burn to the ground in 1936.

The Great Exhibition inspired a series of World's Fairs across the globe. Not to be outdone, America entered itself onto this list with New York's Exhibition of the Industry of All Nations. By coincidence, it opened on Bastille Day (July 14th) in 1853. By further coincidence, it erected a similar glass and iron structure called "The New York Crystal Palace." Naturally, that Crystal Palace also burned to the ground (in 1858).

Philadelphia hosted the first official World's Fair held in the United States. In perhaps a nod to marketing thematic tie-ins, the "Centennial International Exhibition" of 1876 marked the 100th anniversary of the signing of the Declaration of Independence in the city of the original scene. It opened on May 10th and closed on November 10th. During those six months, approximately 10 million people visited the exposition. America's next World's Fair would be even bigger.

The year 1892 would mark the 400th anniversary of Columbus' discovery of America. Here was a milestone that marked the merger of two worlds. It was a marketer's dream. And the United States was selected as the venue to celebrate. Four American cities vied to host: Chicago, New York City, St. Louis, and Washington, D.C. In the end, it was decided to hold the World's Columbian Exposition in the city of Chicago.

The Chicago World's Fair occurred from May 1, 1893 through October 30, 1893. Its array of exhibits (including the first Ferris Wheel) defined American Exceptionalism. With more than 27 million visitors, it became the new standard for World's Fairs. Among the food popularized at the Chicago World's Fair were Cream of Wheat, Juicy Fruit Gum, Shredded Wheat, and, thanks to former slave turned spokeswoman Nancy Green, Aunt Jemima's Pancake Flour.

As we've seen, such was the anticipation of the Chicago World's Fair that the Menches Brothers enlisted their business neighbor and friend William McKinley to help them secure a spot for their concession business. Frank Menches later said, despite McKinley's efforts, "We didn't get the Chicago concession. It went to a Chicago man who had a pull with the fair management."[1] Things would be different by the time of the next official World's Fair in America.

Before we get to that, it's worth mentioning the Pan-American Exposition. Though billed as a "World's Fair," it focused on the Americas – north and south. With a narrower definition of "world" and no real anniversary tie-in, the 1901 Pan-Am Exposition held in Buffalo, N.Y., (at the time America's 8th largest city), still managed to attract more than 8 million attendees. Featuring the benefits of cheap hydro-electric power, its display also attracted the Lackawanna Steel Company to move from Scranton, Pennsylvania to the shores of Lake Erie south of Buffalo.

Yet, it doesn't appear the Menches were particularly interested in attending. Perhaps that's because they were engrossed in Summit Lake Park, which they were expanding to include baseball fields just as the Pan-Am Expo was starting.[2] In addition, they invested in frequent – sometimes daily – advertising of their "Best in Vaudeville" list of acts performing at Summit Lake Park.[3] By September of 1901, the Menches Brothers and the rest of the nation had other concerns.

Without the marketing advantages of the Chicago World's Fair, it would have been difficult for Buffalo's Pan-Am Exposition to meet, let alone exceed, the success of the Windy City's event. Unfortunately, what many remember about the 1901 Pan-Am Expo is the September 6th assassination of President William McKinley. It forever mars the event and, to this day, hangs on every Buffalonian's wall of dishonor in the same way "wide right" rings infamously for every Buffalo Bills fan. The Menches brothers mourned the loss of their friend. Years later Frank would remember him as "one of the finest men I ever knew."[4]

Even as the nation coped with the sad incident in Buffalo, planners were working on the United States' next official World's Fair. The process actually began five years earlier on June 7, 1896 at the monthly meeting of the St. Louis Business Men's League. On that day, during lunch, member David R. Francis, offered the following proposal: "There is one event in the history of this city second in importance to the Declaration of Independence… and that is the Louisiana Purchase."[5]

Francis' proclamation set in motion what eventually became the Louisiana Purchase Exposition, (a.k.a. "The St. Louis World's Fair").

The St. Louis World's Fair from April 30, 1904 through December 1, 1904, ran a month longer than the other expositions. It attracted just under 20 million visitors. St. Louis hosted the 1904 Summer Olympics during the Fair. It was the first time the international games were held in the United States. Not many people remember those games, but they remember the World's Fair.

Despite showing less attendance than the Chicago World's Fair a decade earlier, the St. Louis World's Fair seems to have retained a luster unparalleled in American World's Fairs (although the art deco "world of tomorrow" displayed at the 1939/40 New York World's Fair offers stiff competition). So much of today's culture – especially our food culture – seems to trace itself back to the 1904 St. Louis World's Fair. It's attained almost mythical proportions.

For instance, in terms of well-known foods and beverages, the following are all associated with the St. Louis World's Fair: the ice cream cone, Iced Tea, hot dogs, Dr. Pepper, peanut butter, the club sandwich, the pickle, the kumquat, the grapefruit, the scone, ginseng, the black olive, the fruit icicle (known now by the brand name "Popsicle"), flavored coffees, an early predecessor of the fruit smoothie, "Fairy Floss" (what today we call "cotton candy"), puffed rice, Campbell Soup, and even sliced bread.[6] Oh, yeah, let's not forget the hamburger.

Pamela Vaccaro's comprehensive book *Beyond the Ice Cream Cone – The Whole Scoop on Food at the 1904 World's Fair* (Enid Press, 2004) tackles the truths of these food claims on at least the surface level (and more for certain foods). For example, Vaccaro points out the Pullman Dining Car Service (remember them?) listed "Iced Tea" on its menu. In fact, the folks assigned to prepare the St. Louis World's Fair likely saw this menu as they rode the train on the way to visit the 1901 Pan-Am Exposition in Buffalo.[7]

The mistruth is more blatant with the hot dog. Vacarro states the typical story says that concessionaire Anton Feuchtwanger sold the first hot dog on a bun at the 1904 St. Louis World's Fair. She says it's true that Feuchtwanger is recognized as the first to marry the bun and the hot dog, but he did it in 1883, not 1904![8]

In many cases, the St. Louis World's Fair did play an important role in popularizing certain products. Dr. Pepper and the scone fall into this category. The Campbell Soup baby-faced kids premiered at the 1904 St. Louis World's Fair and have appeared on the company's soup labels ever since.[9]

In addition, some local or regional foods gained national prominence. Florida's "pommel" (what we now call a "grapefruit"), California's flavored coffees, kumquat, and black (ripened) olives, as well as Texas' ginseng can be counted among these.[10]

One item that definitely appears to have debuted at the 1904 St. Louis World's Fair is cotton candy. Marketed as "Fairy Floss," the Electric Candy Machine Company of Nashville, Tennessee operated 200 machines of their "Electric Fairy Floss Candy Spinner" at the Exposition.[11] This new invention was made in late 1903 and had not yet received its trademark until June of 1904. In fact, the company made its filing on May 24th of that year as the St. Louis Fair was being held.[12]

It's odd that, for all the evidence that cotton candy really was "invented" at the 1904 St. Louis World's Fair, it's not even the second most recognized item associated with the Fair. The top honor goes to the ice cream cone (with the hamburger coming in second). There are just too many versions of the ice cream cone invention story to mention here (perhaps enough to fill another book?). Suffice it to say, it's unlikely the cone was actually invented at the fair. Still, never let the facts get in the way of a good story.

Alas, as John Ford most fabulously sculpted in the penultimate scene of *The Man Who Shot Liberty Valance*, "When the legend becomes fact, print the legend." Is this also the case with the role of the St. Louis World's Fair when it comes to serving the first hamburger? Did the inventive skills of an "unknown food vender"[13] on the Fair's "pike" (i.e., midway) really launch the trillion-dollar business we see today?

Well, if we're going to talk Texas-sized big, then we may as well go to Texas itself. And that's where our final suspect resides, as you'll find out in the next chapter.

Chapter Seven:
Fletcher "Old Dave" Davis

If the 1893 Chicago World's Fair symbolized American Exceptionalism, Texas represents the American Individual. Inaugural Cowboy Hall of Famer and Texan Charles Goodnight, who was the first to blaze a cattle trail from the Texas panhandle to New Mexico embodies this very ethos of the Lone Star State.

Will Rogers, a member of that same Hall of Fame class, stands alongside Goodnight as a trailblazer, albeit as a multi-talented entertainer. His performances ranged from the athletic prowess of cowboy rodeos to the physical comedy of vaudeville. An acclaimed humorist, he was a popular speaker who penned more than 4,000 columns syndicated in newspapers across the nation. He also appeared in 71 movies – 50 silent films and 21 (in the then new) "talkies." There's no question at least some of these were shown at the Menches Brothers' Liberty Theater.

But the standout rugged individualist of that initial group of Cowboy Hall of Fame inductees has to be Theodore Roosevelt. Known for his "bully" behavior, he began life as a weak, sickly child. Disregarding the doctor's advice that there was no cure for his asthma, he undertook a strict regimen of physical exercise to improve his health. To overcome his feeble disposition, after being beaten by two older boys, he found a boxing coach so he could learn to defend himself.

Home schooled and self-taught, Roosevelt went to Harvard College. In his sophomore year Roosevelt would suffer the first of several distressing losses when his father died at the young age of 46. He directed his full focus to his studies, eventually graduating *magna cum laude*. On his twenty-second birthday he married socialite Alice Hathaway Lee of Chestnut Hill, Massachusetts. She was 19 years old.

While at Harvard, Roosevelt began researching what would ultimately become his first book, *The Naval War of 1812*. The widely acclaimed and very readable volume was published in 1882, the same year he upset the incumbent Assemblyman in New York's 21st District. Roosevelt was only twenty-four years old. The following year he become Minority Leader of the State Assembly. As impressive as these achievements were, none of them earned him inclusion in the Cowboy Hall of Fame. What happened next, however, did.

Valentine's Day, 1884, would forever change Theodore Roosevelt's life. It was on that afternoon, two days after giving birth to their first child, a birth from which she would never recover, Alice Roosevelt died in the arms of her husband. She was only twenty-two.

Making matters worse, a few hours earlier, Roosevelt's mother succumbed to Typhoid Fever. He would write this entry into his diary on this fateful day: "The light has gone out of my life."

Distraught, Roosevelt left his daughter (with his sister), he left the Assembly, and he left the state of New York. He went west. He went to the Badlands of Dakota. It's a region known for its hot summers and cold winters. He settled in what is now the city of Medora, North Dakota. Today we might say he went there, forlorn and alone, to find himself. He succeeded.

His tenacity and eventual mastery of cowboy skills didn't necessarily awe the real working cowboys of Dakota, but it did command a certain amount of admiration. Although his tenure in Dakota Territory would last only a short time, the raw masculinity it engendered contrasted nicely to Roosevelt's rightfully earned, though stultifying, intellectual persona. How Roosevelt responded to the premature death of his young wife helped propel him to higher accomplishments, (though there would be one final heartache towards the end of his life).

Theodore Roosevelt wasn't the only young man attracted to Dakota. The skies were clear and the weather pleasant in Rochelle, Illinois on Friday, September 14, 1884. As the parade snaked from the depot to the fairgrounds, several dozen young women, one for each state, sat in a large wagon following the marching bands. Last among them, by herself on the platform extending from the rear of the cart, sat the pretty face of Dakota territory. Among the many spectators lining the streets along the parade route were "hundreds of young men whose eyes followed the face while they shouted and cheered for Dakota."[1] The thermometer hovered in the upper sixties in Rochelle. Further down south in St. Louis it was pleasant with afternoon temperatures rising into the high 70s.[2] That same weekend, in the city of Carrollton, Illinois, just north of St. Louis, a young couple married.

Fletcher Short Davis, born in Winchester, Illinois on October 6, 1864, was twenty-three years old when he married Alice Jane McCracken on September 14, 1888.[3] She was 19 years old.

Nothing stands out in the historical record regarding the Davis family. For the next three years, they presumably led the kind of life one would expect from young families. Their first son, Will Vere Davis, was born on July 25, 1890. Two years later, on May 8, 1892, Alice gave birth to their second son, H. D. "Dow" Davis.

But then something happened. Just four months after Dow came into this world, Alice left it. Alice Davis died on September 25, 1892. She was only twenty-two.

Distraught, Davis left his two boys (with his in-laws), left Carrollton, and left the state of Illinois. He went west. He went to East Texas. It's a region known for its hot summers and cold winters (albeit not as cold as the Badlands). He settled in what is now the city of Athens, Texas. Today we might say he went there, forlorn and alone, to find himself. He succeeded.

It's quite possible Davis might have followed in the footsteps of McKendree Miller. Like Davis, Miller came from Illinois. He worked in the pottery business in Louisiana and Missouri before relocating to Athens, Texas in 1884. In February of 1885, he founded Athens Pottery. Miller's sons, Elmer and Pearl Eli Miller, eventually took over the business.[4] (Joseph) Elmer was born in 1866[5] and Pearl was born in 1869,[6] so they'd be close to Davis in age.

If Davis had struck up a friendship with one of the Miller boys, that might have led him to Athens. We know he landed a job at Athens Pottery soon after his arrival in Athens. He later became a brick mason and contractor. He married Racilla A. Allison on November 28, 1896.[7] "Siddy" (or "Ciddy," it's spelled both ways), was the sister of Ambrosia "Brosia" Allison Miller.[8] Brosia was the wife of Pearl Miller.[9] According to an interview with Kindree Miller, Pearl and Brosia's son, Davis wrote Pearl for a job as a pottery turner.[10] It's possible Pearl not only gave Davis a job, but he may have also introduced him to his future wife.

Affectionately known as "Old Dave" or "Uncle Fletch," his eldest son eventually followed him to Texas. Davis had a keen interest in athletics, particularly baseball, as well as Republican politics.[11] He didn't get quite as far as Theodore Roosevelt, but they did share one final similarity. His youngest son died at age 26 while serving in the first World War. He was killed in France on November 4, 1918, just a week before the Armistice was signed that ended the war.[12]

Only a few months earlier, on Bastille Day, seven German Fokker Chasse planes intercepted a group of four allied Nieuport 28 fighter planes that had crossed the lines looking for Boche Observation machines. In the ensuing dogfight, each side lost a plane and the pilot within it. The America pilot's name was Quentin Roosevelt, Teddy's youngest son. He was but four years old when Roosevelt ascended to the presidency. His impish behavior earned him the moniker "my fine bad little boy." A favorite of his father, Roosevelt called Quentin and his handful of friends the "White House Gang." Some say Theodore Roosevelt never recovered from this loss. He died in his sleep seven months later. Yet, even in death, the Lone Star Spirit survived. Then Vice President, Thomas R. Marshall, said, "Death had to take Roosevelt sleeping, for if he had been awake, there would have been a fight."

Fletcher Davis was a fighter, too. On Thursday, March 7, 1940, he suffered a heart attack. He was awake when it happened. He fought relentlessly. He remained vibrant as late as Sunday afternoon, as he sat up without effort. He talked with the friends that visited him. That evening, though, within minutes after going to bed, he passed away. Like Roosevelt, death took Davis while he slept.[13]

Legend has it Fletcher "Old Dave" Davis flipped the first burger while working a side job at a luncheonette during the slow periods at Athens Pottery. There are those who are convinced he was the mysterious "unknown food vender" interviewed at the 1904 St. Louis World's Fair, so the Fletcher Davis hamburger origin story is intertwined with the St. Louis World's Fair hamburger origin story. Will these two seemingly independent threads bind the truth more tightly? Or will it expose contradictions that ultimately unravels both their tales?

Now that we've identified the prime suspects, you're probably left wondering about the unanswered question: Why do we have so many claims? The purpose behind the suspects' stories can reveal much. We shall disclose these motives in our next chapter. Before you turn the page, though, here's a clue: There are two classes of motives: those evolving from modern events and those stemming from contemporaneous events. Which of these motives will be the most telling?

CHAPTER EIGHT:
DON'T RAIN ON OUR HOMETOWN FESTIVAL

Having established our list of suspects, we can now move on to the next stage of discovery. You may recognize the fruits of this as the "means, motive, and opportunity" summation presented by the trial attorney in any typical TV courtroom drama. Two of these three elements are measurable – means and opportunity. The third – motive – assumes we know what the suspect is thinking.

How are each of these elements defined?

Means is "the instrument or agency through which an end or purpose is accomplished." This includes the ready availability of any resources required to carry out the task.[1] Clearly all our suspects have the means to flip a burger, especially the three that were in the food-selling business (i.e., the Menches Brothers, Charles Nagreen, and Louis Lassen).

Opportunity is the "situation in which the commitment of resources may lead to unforeseen gains."[2] Again, all, to one extent or another, were placed in circumstances to flip those burgers. As with means, though, Fletcher Davis was in the weakest position in terms of opportunity, but there's no reason to believe he never had the opportunity.

Motive refers to "why one committed the crime, the inducement, reason, or willful desire and purpose behind the commission of an offense." It should be noted that "whether the purpose was good, like helping someone commit suicide, or bad, like committing murder, it is not a deciding factor in deciding guilt or innocence. But, intent is."[3]

Let's digress for a moment and look at intent. Intent "shows the presence of will in the act which consummates a crime."[4] It's willful and premeditated. We can find no evidence in the contemporaneous records (i.e., newspaper articles published at the time any of the hamburger origin stories point to) that suggest any of the suspects deliberately sought to invent the hamburger.

What kind of reporting would we have expected if the selling of the first hamburger was intentional? We need look no further than the invention of cotton candy (as relayed in Chapter 6). Originally called "Fairy Floss," the Electric Candy Machine Company of Nashville, Tennessee purposely sought and obtained a vendor's license to place 200 of their newly invented "Electric Fair Floss Candy Spinner" machines at the 1904 St. Louis World's Fair. That's intent. And it's documented in newspaper articles and the U.S. Trademark office at the same time the event occurred.

In three of the four cases, the invention is described not as intentional but as accidental in nature, the result of unexpected random events. Again, the odd man out is Fletcher Davis, his story is neither intentional nor accidental as it contains no "reason" for him to have created the sandwich.

We can go a step further. Remarkably, for the significant impact the hamburger has today, no contemporaneous credible and objective records appear to be present for any of the suspects. In every case, the hamburger story didn't surface until decades after the actual event.

This fact causes us to return to motive. Why do the stories exist in the first place? What prompted their initial appearance and why do they endure without question today?

To best examine the motives, we will look both at the motives at the time of the original telling of each story (which may answer why they came about) and the current motives (which may answer why they endure).

CONTEMPORANEOUS MOTIVES:

Menches Brothers: As serial entrepreneurs, they thought of marketing from a strategic standpoint. They didn't think in terms of singular products since they had a portfolio of products. Indeed, they had a portfolio of businesses. At the time of initial publicly documented disclosure (1922[5]), they had shed their national and regional businesses but retained several local businesses. From a marketing standpoint, there was nothing to gain and possibly something to lose if they told an origin story that didn't involve local participants as that was the market they were then targeting.

Charles Nagreen: The prototype carnival barker, he thought solely in terms of hawking a single product. Though he had several small businesses, they were all retail oriented (i.e., product sales). He understood the importance of focus in terms of marketing. The product he chose to focus on was the hamburger. He even branded himself as "Hamburger Charlie." You can't get more focused than that. At the time of disclosure (1934[6]) he was still operating the same county fair lunch stand he had always run. The story helped reinforce brand awareness and provided a perpetual publicity device.

Louis Lassen: A traditional retail sales operator, he could afford to sit back and wait for customers. As a result, he never really promoted his hamburger origin story. He just wanted to serve workers lunch. Oddly, when his grandson was running the luncheonette, he purchased advertising in 1950 that stated, "Originators of the steak sandwich."[7] It didn't mention the hamburger, even though it was also on the menu. Apparently, when your restaurant is very small and can't fit a lot of people, there's no motive to do anything that would attract more people.

Fletcher Davis: Those who win the lottery never expect to win the lottery. They just happen to be in the right place at the right time. That's "Old Dave." He just liked making hamburgers for people. Until he didn't (as the story goes). One thing for sure, he never made a big deal about it. At least as far as we can tell from the official record. It's not even mentioned in his obituary.

As you can see, things were pretty quiet in terms of motives from the original suspects. If we skip ahead to the "modern" era, things tend to get a little more exciting, especially in the case of Louis Lassen and Fletcher Davis.

MODERN MOTIVES:

Menches Brothers: In 1985, based on a chapter in the book *Tanbark and Tinsel* by John C. Kunzog, the Chamber of Commerce in the town of Hamburg, New York decided to create an event in honor of the 100th anniversary of the invention of the hamburger. It received plenty of national press coverage. While promotors knew Kunzog named the Menches Brothers as the creators of the new sandwich, they mistakenly thought the boys were local. Ironically, Kunzog says in the book he interviewed Frank Menches at his office in the Liberty Theatre in Akron, Ohio. So much for reading the fine print. Today, both Akron, Ohio and Hamburg, New York have continuing festivities celebrating the birth of the hamburger. Descendants of the Menches family have resurrected their family's hamburger tradition by establishing a restaurant in Akron. Therefore, both the municipalities and the family have a motive to promote the Menches Brothers story.

Charles Nagreen: Not to be outdone by Hamburg, New York, things began cooking in Seymour, Wisconsin in 1989. That year, at the town's first "Home of the Hamburger" Celebration, they cooked the "World's Largest Hamburger" (weighing in at more than 5,000 pounds). Seymour, Wisconsin has since created a community-wide marketing effort that includes festivals, "Home of the Hamburger" documentation, and they've even established the "Hamburger Hall of Fame" in their city. You think they're motivated?

Louis Lassen: While Ken Lassen, Louis' grandson, is quoted in print telling the hamburger story no later than in 1963,[8] the "landmark" significance of the story became critical a few years later. In fact, Louis' Lunch very survival depended on it. In 1965, the City of New Haven decided to create a parking lot on the property where Louis' Lunch was located.[9] Though giving an outward appearance of accommodation, Ken apparently didn't trust either the local or Federal government officials behind this urban renewal initiative. In 1967 he helped Louis' Lunch obtain landmark status from the New Haven Preservation Board based at least in part on its claim to having served the world's first hamburger. To further emphasize the point, he secured a nationally distributed UPI story stating this.[10] Things got progressively worse as the failed parking lot plan was replaced by a proposal to build a medical building. Stating "I do not go without the building," Ken vowed to fight City Hall. The "birthplace of the burger" and "certified landmark" figuring prominently in his story.[11]

The situation became critical in January 1974 when a *New York Times* article reported eviction was "only months away."[12] In March of that year, as all appeared lost, Ken lamented to a reporter, "We have researched this, and the New Haven Conservation Trust and others have checked out work. 1900 is one thing they can't take away from me."[13] A bolt from the blue helped stave off execution when a Nixon administration official cited an Executive Order dealing with "the historicity of the property" in an effort to delay demolition.[14] Ken continued his fight, but the cause was eventually lost. Miraculously, only hours before the final eviction was to take place, Ken bought a small lot a few blocks away and Louis' Lunch was moved lock, stock and barrel in one piece to the location where it remains.[15]

Louis' Lunch survives to this day in part due to the tenacity of Ken Lassen, but not without the help of the Louis Lassen hamburger origin story. How's that for motivation?

Fletcher Davis: When he read the January 1974 *New York Times* article, Dallas Cowboys owner Clint Murchison, Jr. took offense of the Louis' Lunch claim. He decided to do something about it. He called his friend Francis X. "Frank" Tolbert, a columnist at the *Dallas Morning News*.

Clint told Frank the following story: "It seems that before my father was born (in 1895) my Grandfather Murchison regularly ate a wonderful sandwich prepared by an old man named Dave (last name lost to recollection) who served from behind the counter at the J. J. Powers Drug Store, later Stirman's Drug Store, on the courthouse square in Athens.... the sandwich became so appreciated locally that the Athens Chamber of Commerce got together a kitty and sent Dave to the 1904 World's Fair in St. Louis to advertise the city. A fancy dan reporter from the old *New York Tribune* interviewed Dave about his hamburger… about 2 weeks later a story was published in the *New York Tribune* which said that the hamburger sandwich was the idea of a 'food vendor' at the St. Louis Fair."[16]

Murchison's vivid story convinced Tolbert to use his investigative reporting skills to track down the story of the unknown "food vendor" from the St. Louis World's Fair. For more than two years Tolbert did his "sweat-neck" research until he was able to conclude that anonymous "food vendor" at the 1904 St. Louis World's Fair was none other than Fletcher Davis.[17] Once certain of the veracity of his story, he created a burger festival, mimicking the festival he had created earlier for chili. It remains a popular festival today. The festival obviously provides a more than adequate motive for Athens, Texas to continue to stake its claim as the birthplace of the hamburger.

As far as what might have originally motivated Murchison to call Tolbert? We don't have to speculate. Murchison himself told us. He said, "Let's face it; if we let the Yankees get away with claiming the invention of the hamburger, they'll be going after chili con carne next." That's a motive you can sink your teeth into.

*   *   *   *   *

Each of our suspects had the means to sell the first hamburger and they had the opportunity to sell the first hamburger. The municipalities associated with each origins story have, in one form of another, erected a shrine to their chosen champion. This creates a motive to maintain the sanctity of each suspect's account. Can we pinpoint which of the suspects is the guilty party? Can we prove who really sold the first hamburger? We don't want to rain on anyone's parade, so let's go straight to the bottom-line. Unfortunately (or fortunately, depending on the point of view of certain local chambers of commerce), since there is no contemporaneous "smoking gun" evidence, we can have no way of knowing if any of these legends are true…

… or do we? (…continued on the next pages in Act Two: The Investigation.)

Section Two:

– The Investigation –

Eliminate the Impossible

CHAPTER NINE:
HAMBURGER HELPER – SOLVING THE GREATEST
WHODUNIT? IN CULINARY HISTORY

Within the mists of time lie buried uncoverable answers to history's most compelling questions. What really happened to the lost continent of Atlantis? How did ancient Greeks possess the technology to create the Antikythera mechanism and what did they use it for? Why did hundreds of people suddenly start dancing in the streets of Strasbourg during July 1518 and then, just as suddenly, die? Who was Jack the Ripper? And, finally, where did Amelia Earhart end up?

These questions pale to the ultimate mystery. It's the mystery behind something that has touched us all and will continue to touch generations into the future. It's the mystery behind a trillion-dollar industry. It's the mystery behind something so simple, so common, so obvious, that no one bothered to write it down. It is, the birth of the world's first hamburger.

Did the 1904 World's Fair in St. Louis really inaugurate the "hamburg sandwich" as purportedly described in a *New York Tribune* article that same year and as said to be taught by McDonald's famous Hamburger University?

Or was the first hamburger served in 1900 at Louis' Lunch, a diner in New Haven, Connecticut as reported by the *New York Times* and recognized as such by the Library of Congress?

Or did Fletcher "Old Dave" Davis first place a ground beef patty on bread in "the late 1880's" as suggested by the *Dallas Morning News*?

And, if the hamburger really was first invented in 1885 either by Charles Nagreen at the Outagamie County Fair in Seymour, Wisconsin, or by Charles and Frank Menches at the Erie County Fair in Hamburg, New York, which fair occurred first?

Join us now as we explore these various origin stories and use classic crime solving techniques to crack one of history's greatest culinary whodunits.

in...

THE SHRINE OF THE FOUR...
(AND A HALF?).

CHAPTER TEN:
IDENTIFY THE WEAPON

"You will not apply my precept," he said, shaking his head. *"How often have I said to you that when you have eliminated the impossible, whatever remains, however improbable, must be the truth?"*

Thus spoke crime fighting sleuth Sherlock Holmes in *The Sign of the Four*, Sir Arthur Conan Doyle's second novel featuring his most-popular character, as published in the February 1890 issue of *Lippincott's Monthly Magazine*. By coincidence, the most noted hamburger origin stories occurred within a few years on either side of this date. It's fitting, then, that we employ the deductive techniques of the Baker Street mastermind in attempting to solve one of history's greatest culinary mysteries: Who sold the first hamburger?

Before we can do this, though, we need to focus on the "weapon." In this case, it's the sandwich itself.

Perhaps it's best to start at the end of the story.

Let's begin with those fascinating evenings in the 1950s and 1960s when American families dined in front of the soft fluorescent glow of small cabinets emitting black and white images. On special occasions, or when mom (who did most of the cooking back then) was just plumb tuckered out, parents treated their kids to TV Dinners.

In 1954, just as many Americans were adding televisions to their living room furniture complement, C.A. Swanson & Co. coined the term "TV Dinner" to brand its pre-packaged frozen food line. The first meals included chicken, turkey, and beef offerings. In the latter category, it was the "Salisbury steak" option that quickly became a favorite. Perhaps you remember bugging your mother to buy one for you.

Salisbury steak stood out as the jewel of all TV Dinners. It was the luxury of luxuries, topped with mushrooms and smothered in a rich, tasty, gravy. Who could forget how your mouth salivated with anticipation as your fork gently cut a bite-sized piece from this fancy meat cake. This wasn't your mother's meatloaf. It was a meal fit for a king.

And it wasn't a hamburger. If you wanted a quick hamburger, you asked your parents to take you to White Castle or McDonald's or Burger King or (eventually) Wendy's. If you wanted a quick steak, you'd ask for Salisbury steak.

"Salisbury." Even its name connotes the aristocratic flair of England's House of Lords if not the royalty of Buckingham Palace itself. Indeed, according to a King Features syndicated column, "It is named in honor of the third Marquis of Salisbury, once Prime Minister of England."[1] Something to do about Queen Victoria not liking the smell of onions and the Marquis creating a culinary dish to meet his Queen's nasal requirements.

Of course, none of this is true. (Why would you believe anything you read in the newspaper?) The true story of Salisbury steak is far more interesting – and more American. Furthermore, if you are a fan, you might be interested to know those tasty Salisbury steaks in your frozen dinners bear no resemblance to the original Salisbury steak.

At his country home in Dobbs Ferry, New York, overlooking the eastern shore of the Hudson River, Dr. James H. Salisbury died on Wednesday, August 23, 1905. Just two months shy of his eighty-second birthday, the *New York Tribune* and *New York Times* wrote admiring obituaries highlighting his well-regarded contributions in the study of chronic diseases and his ground-breaking work in germ theory.[2,3] Neither mentioned his famous Salisbury diet, the therapy treatment that spawned what became known as Salisbury steak and is considered one of America's notable dietary fads.[4]

The Salisbury diet consists of consuming nothing more than hot water and "Salisbury steak." In an 1885 medical publication, a W.M. Hepburn, M.D., from Freehold, New Jersey offered preparation instructions as follows:

> "The Salisbury steak is made by taking the best slices of the 'round' of the beef, and chopping it with dull knives. The object is not to cut, but rather pound the meat...

On pounding the meat, as directed, the pulp comes to the top, and the tough, fibrous portion remains below. This pulp is scraped off and made into cakes — like sausage-cakes — or in shape like a good-sized steak, and gently broiled on a gridiron. It has been found that meat gently cooked is more digestible than raw. The fire must be good, so that the meat may be rapidly broiled — that is, be cooked on the outside and almost raw inside. A little salt and pepper and a small amount of butter added makes a not at all unpalatable dish, and one which contains all the strength of the beef, with the tough, indigestible portion entirely separated."[5]

Much heralded in its heyday, as with all fads the Salisbury diet received radiant accounts: "Salisbury steak appears to be giving remarkably good results as a diet for people troubled with weak or disordered digestion."[6] "One of the new wrinkles is to feed people whose stomachs are out of kilter on 'Salisbury steak.'"[7] Within a year of these lead sentences, however, reports began appearing that suggested the "famed Salisbury diet" wasn't the panacea it had been made out to be.[8]

Just shy of a decade after Dr. Hepburn's recipe appeared, the press was calling Dr. James H. Salisbury "a crank, the prince of quacks," and declared, "The fad, as a fad, died out."[9] Of his famed Salisbury steak, one reporter wrote it was "a most insipid unappetizing dish, and greatly lacking in nourishment. It looks like dog vomit, and tastes like – nothing…"[10]

Now, if you're a culinary aficionado, you might begin to suspect James Salisbury may have simply usurped and relabeled another dish that was growing in popularity at the same time: the Hamburg steak. The story goes that Dr. Salisbury came up with his treatment while serving as a doctor in the Civil War, and his own marketing brochure stated he "has been in business since 1863."[11] On the other hand, in no later than the summer of 1872, Thorpe's, "a quiet way-side hostelrie" about fourteen miles from San Francisco "just beyond San Bruno station on the San Jose railroad" served "Hamburg steak" for breakfast.[12] The following summer in 1873, at Anderson's European Hotel at 143 & 145 East Madison Street (between Clark and LaSalle), a room would cost you $1 to $2 per day, but a "Hamburg steak" cost you only thirty cents.[13]

In neither case are we told exactly what a "Hamburg" steak is. In 1880, however, it was reported the Hamburg Steak arrived in Lincoln, Nebraska as "a new dish prepared only by the Rialto, for a few special German friends. It consists of chopped steak seasoned with pepper, salt, and onions, and served without being even warmed."[14] Similarly, a recipe appeared in a Minnesota newspaper that read like this: "Hamburg Steak – Cut or pound round steak to make it tender, spread it with fried onions, fold again and beat; this is, for those who like onions, a delicious breakfast dish, and easily prepared. In greasing the gridiron for broiling rub with a bit of leaf fat; this is always well to do, it does not mar the flavor, and it does not waste as butter does."[15] Both descriptions sound very similar to a Salisbury steak, only without the onions (which may have inspired the false "Marquis of Salisbury" story described earlier).

Complicating matters is a food known as "Hamburger steak." This may or may not have been just a different name for "Hamburg steak," although its German origins are clearer. It has been described as a "beef cheese" (a spiced mince-meat left in a cloth bag overnight[16]), a dish served raw,[17] or merely "hash."[18] By the summer of 1885, "Hamburger steak" had evolved into what was commonly referred to as "Hamburg steak," as newspapers began reprinting this recipe originally published in *The Philadelphia Caterer*:

> "In the first place the steak itself must be good. Any economy practiced in this respect toward the Hamburger will be just as fatal to its excellence as to that of any other mode of cooking a steak. A good sirloin or a good rump, entirely free from any stringiness, should be used, and the proportion of fat to lean to please most tastes would probably be one fourth, or perhaps a little less of the form and three fourths of the latter. The meat should be minced very finely, and seasoned thus: For each half pound of the meat add two teaspoonfuls of finely minced

onion, a half of a clove of garlic also chopped very fine, and pepper and salt, a half a teaspoonful of each of the two latter would probably suit most palates. After the seasoning is thoroughly mixed through it, the meat is to be formed into rather thin cakes and fried on both sides in butter, the pan, of course, being thoroughly heated before the meat is put in; when done, dish up and serve with the gravy poured over it, garnishing with Lyonnaise potatoes. Many persons may object to the addition of garlic and onion, and the steak can, of course, be prepared without them; yet in that case it is hardly entitled to the name of Hamburger."[19]

It would, though, have been entitled to the name of "Salisbury" (assuming you held the gravy).

So, which came first? The Salisbury or the Hamburg steak? Although attempts were made to keep the two distinct,[20,21] by 1911 it was clear the only difference between the two was the lack of onions in Salisbury steak.[22] In fact, as a subset of Hamburg steak, the term "Salisbury steak" may have died off completely if it had not been for World War I. The hostilities in Europe brought such distaste for the Germans that restaurants across America joined in Patriotic unison. In place of "Hamburg steak," "Salisbury steak" began appearing on menus. When asked what this new listing was, a Kansas waiter replied, "It is what used to be called 'Hamburger steak' before the war."[23] Was there a difference in preparation? A Boston writer said, "They taste alike to me, but one has an English name, the other a German name, and they both went through a Yankee meat-chopper."[24] The name change even crossed the border when dining cars in Canada stopped listing "Hamburger steaks" and began listing "Salisbury steaks."[25]

By 1923, the recipe for Salisbury steak – the one we've come to know and love via TV Dinners – and the recipe for the Hamburg steak had become the same – with the onions being optional.[26] To the extent there was a difference, Salisbury steaks were considered "a bit more aristocratic,"[27] and that impression is the one that appears to have stuck, at least in the minds of young baby boomers.

Those are the same young minds that knew the difference between Salisbury steak and hamburgers.

How does this bear on our identification of the weapon in our mystery?

The trouble is, sometimes a new creation is not named until it becomes popular enough to merit a name. As a result, what we today call a "hamburger" may also have been originally called a "Hamburger sandwich," "Hamburger steak sandwich," or a "Hamburg steak sandwich." The fact we have a dish, made from very similar ingredients, called "Hamburg steak" and "Hamburger steak" can trick you. We need to define a clear difference.

The distinguishing difference comes down to this one word: "sandwich."

Late nineteenth century recipes for "Hamburg steak/Hamburger steak" call for steak to be minced, mixed with egg and formed in various shapes before frying in butter and served on a plate covered in gravy. This is not a sandwich. This is an entrée served on a dish. You eat a Hamburg steak with a knife and a fork while sitting at a table. You eat a hamburger like you eat any other sandwich – with your hands and often while standing or walking. A Hamburg steak, therefore, is clearly not a hamburger.

Ergo, our weapon must be the sandwich, not the steak.

The similarity of the names may confuse us today, but it certainly didn't confuse people back then. The menu of the American Restaurant in Manila contains a listing for a "Hamburg sandwich" and a separate listing for a "Hamburg steak." You might note the steak costs more than twice as much as the sandwich.[28]

They served Hamburg steaks in California no later than 1872. Clearly, this entrée appeared on restaurant menus before then. (But not at Delmonico's in 1834 as a notoriously fake menu purports.[29]) What's the earliest recorded instance of someone serving a hamburger sandwich? The answer to that question begins our Sherlock Holmes-like quest to eliminate the impossible. We take the first steps in that journey right now…

CHAPTER ELEVEN:
HAMBURGERS – THE WRITTEN RECORD

Armed with our weapon – the hamburger sandwich – and having identified our leading suspects, we thus begin the Holmesian method to "eliminate the impossible." We need not know anything more about our suspects than the date of their claim. If we can find a reference to a hamburger sandwich (in any of its various names) prior to that date, then we can deduce it's impossible that suspect could have served the first hamburger.

As in all good police thrillers, let's again run down our line-up of suspects (in reverse chronological order). In each case of the individuals named, their hometowns have created what amounts to a shrine to their claims. We count them as four and a half because two are inexorably tangled together. Still, for our purposes we'll untie them. Here's the line-up:

Suspect #½: **An Unknown Vendor at the St. Louis World's Fair**
Location: St. Louis, Missouri
Year of Claim: 1904
Attributed Initial Source: *New York Tribune* article (1904)

Suspect #1: **Louis Lassen of Louis' Lunch**
Location: New Haven, Connecticut
Year of Claim: 1900
Initial Source: *The Yale Daily News* article (1963)

Suspect #2: **Fletcher "Old Dave" Davis (the "Unknown Vendor" at the St. Louis World's Fair)**
Location: Athens, Texas
Year of Claim: "Late 1880s"
Initial Source: Frank Tolbert, *Dallas Morning News* column (1976)

Suspect #3: Charles "Hamburger Charlie" Nagreen
Location: Outagamie County Fair, Seymour, Wisconsin
Year of Claim: 1885
Initial Source: *The Post-Crescent* article (1934), *Green Bay Press-Gazette* article (1937)

Suspect #4: Frank and Charles Menches
Location: Erie County Fair, Hamburg, New York
Year of Claim: 1885
Initial Source: 1920s Interview relayed in Chapter 11 of *Tanbark and Tinsel*, by John C. Kunzog (1970)

That's the line-up. Take a close look at them. Remember the earlier chapters that described who they were as people, where their lives led them, and how their hamburger origin stories emerged. These are all important clues in solving our mystery.

[Author's Note: With all due respect to our friends in Tulsa, Oklahoma, the list of suspects omits Oscar Weber Bilby for two reasons. The Bilby stories first appeared in 1995 after then Oklahoma Governor Frank Keating proclaimed Tulsa to be the birthplace of the hamburger. The story however, did not claim Bilby invented the hamburger sandwich. He was merely the first person to put the burger on the bun. Second, the initial event was said to have occurred at a family picnic on Bilby's farm on July 4, 1891.[1] Bilby, therefore, was not selling hamburgers; thus, he does not qualify as a suspect. It should be noted that the family opened a restaurant in June 1933 that still operates today. It features Oscar's original root beer as well as the iron grill he forged in 1891, upon which he cooked those hamburgers that eventually found their place on buns made by his wife Fanny.[2]]

The best (and easiest) manner to "eliminate the impossible" is to access digitized records of periodicals and newspapers. Fortunately, several free resources exist (should you decide to play this game in the comfort of your own home): The Library of Congress's "Chronicling America" archive of historic American newspapers, FultonHistory.com, and the historic New York newspapers web-site. In addition, the subscription-based site Newspapers.com contains digitized newspapers over and above what's available from the free resources. With this record of history at our fingertips, we are now ready to proceed in the footsteps of Sir Arthur Conan Doyle's celebrated detective.

Here's how the "eliminate the impossible" method works: Pick a suspect; Identify the date the suspect allegedly sold the first hamburger; and, Search the database of old newspapers to see if there's a mention of someone selling a hamburger prior to that date.

Let's start by focusing on our first suspect: The Louisiana Purchase Exposition, a.k.a., "The St. Louis World's Fair." This event occurred from April 30th, 1904 through December 1st, 1904. If the hamburger were truly invented at this event by "an unknown vendor," we should see no published record of a "hamburger sandwich" prior to that date.

It just so happens there's an advertisement for a diner called The New Lunch Room in the Friday, April 22, 1904 issue of *The Poultney Journal.* The advertisement in this Vermont newspaper featured the restaurant's menu. The top of the list reads "Hamburg Sandwich….. 10 cents."[3] This appeared a week before the St. Louis World's Fair even started. Clearly, the hamburger was not invented at the Fair in St. Louis in 1904.

This isn't necessarily breaking news. Other historians and reporters have previously uncovered this fact (see Chapter 13 "It's the Sizzle that Sells, Not the Steak" for more details). Fans of the St. Louis World's Fair offer two counterpoints. First, you might hear them say, "We might not have invented the hamburger, but we're the place where the hamburger was first placed on a bun." This is also not true. Two years before the St. Louis event, the Elk's Jubilee carnival in Davenport, Iowa boasted "One Hamburger sandwich man disposed of 400 buns to hungry pedestrians Thursday, and yet he remarked that business was very dull."[4] Sorry, St. Louis, you can't claim the "hamburger on a bun" idea, either. (Although this doesn't eliminate Oscar Weber Bilby from contention.)

Still, the St. Louis advocates remain steadfast. "At least we're the place that popularized the hamburger." This may be a bit subjective. While there are contemporary reports of this, as early as 1900 the popularity of "red-hot hamburger sandwiches" caused a ruckus in Princeton, Indiana.[5] In response to "the small army of hamburg sandwich men which has sprung up in this city," uptown restaurant owners presented a signed petition and presented it to the city council.[6]

Three strikes and you're out, St. Louis. The 1904 World's Fair may have spawned the first strands of cotton candy and launched this now standard carnival delight to prominence. It, however, had nothing to do with propelling the hamburger to stardom. That ship had already sailed.

Because the written record reveals hamburger sandwiches were sold prior to the opening of the Louisiana Purchase Exposition, it is impossible for the first hamburger to have been sold there. We must, therefore, eliminate the 1904 St. Louis World's Fair from our list of suspects.

But wait. There's more.

Your eyes might have noticed the events in Princeton, Indiana occurred in the year "1900." That's the same year as Louis Lassen's claim to have sold the first hamburger. Louis' Lunch accumulated plenty of affidavits to attest to this event. It was enough to convince the New Haven Preservation Trust to bestow "Landmark status" on the original restaurant in 1967.[7] Now, the Louis' Lunch origin story never had a fixed date, so there's no way of knowing if Lassen's inventive act preceded the fight in Princeton. Problems reached their height in Indiana in September, so that would give Louis Lassen about three-quarters of a year to have flopped his steak trimmings onto toast.

Unless…

Unfortunately for those offering testimony, the historical record does not support Louis' Lunch claim to be the first establishment to serve a hamburger. Harper and Jones, an Omaha, Nebraska restaurant, placed several ads in the *Iowa State Bystander* beginning in September of 1899. Their "Hamburg Sandwich" was listed for only five cents.[8] Omaha must have been a happening place for hamburg sandwiches in 1899. In November of that year, William Hansen got whacked in the head with Ed Sutton's crutch after Hansen started arguing over the price of the hamburger sandwich he just bought from a late-night lunch wagon.[9]

These late-night lunch wagons seemed to have generated their fair share of crime stories. Besides Nebraska, we see evidence of crimes associated with these venues involving hamburger sandwiches from Indiana,[10] Kentucky,[11] and Missouri.[12] Granted, the Kentucky story dealt with the last meal of a condemned murderer.

In general, though, lunch wagons received quite favorable press. The mining town of Bisbee, Arizona rejoiced when a new lunch wagon appeared.[13] The joy was short-lived. Ten days later, a man came after the wagon's owner with a gun. The wagon owner skipper town. The wagon stayed, but, for hungry customers, the new proprietor could not "make those famous hot-stuff hamburger-sandwiches and so is unable to tickle their palates as they are want to have them tickled."[14]

That same year (1896), Chicago glorified the "Sandwich Car." The fare of this particular lunch wagon included "a distinguished favorite, only five cents each, is Hamburger steak sandwich, the meat for which is kept ready in small patties and 'cooked while you wait on the gasoline range.'"[15]

One of the earliest newspaper accounts of a hamburger comes from the Monday, July 23, 1894 edition of the *San Francisco Chronicle*. A feature article on page seven tells the complete story of how hamburgers are made. Beneath the headline ("Odors of the Onion – A New Night Feature of City Life – Breezes Pregnant With the Hamburger – How Curbstone Chefs Dispense Fragrant Food From Their Little Carts.") you'll even find illustrations of the "chef" flipping two hamburgers at once and a satisfied patron eating the burger as he walks from the cart.[16]

With this last example, we now see proof that lunch wagons sold hamburger sandwiches before Louis Lassen launched his own lunch wagon on the streets of New Haven in 1895. Louis' grandson, when the loss of the restaurant was imminent, once said of his grandfather's "invention" of the hamburger, "1900 is one thing they can't take away from me."[17] Alas, history has taken away this claim. What can never be taken away, however, is Ken Lassen's tireless and ultimately successful fight with city hall. For that, it's Ken, not Louis, that stands among the pantheon of all-American heroes.

Possibly the earliest reference to selling hamburgers comes from a saloon in Reno, Nevada. In 1893, the establishment of Parry & Evans apparently had a very good knack for publicity. When Tom Fraker arrived to open its new lunch counter, he boldly stated he "prides himself on his ability to make hamburger sandwiches."[18] It was said of Tom that his "celebrated Hamburger steak sandwiches are always on hand to replenish an empty stomach and even fortify Satan himself."[19]

That the journalists of Reno, Nevada spoke of "hamburger sandwiches" without explanation suggests the product was already well understood by 1893. It therefore must have been served elsewhere. It may just be that the periodicals that wrote of these earlier events have yet to be digitized.

Before we leave this chapter, it's incumbent to address a few common misperceptions regarding who sold the first hamburger. One of the most challenging aspects of this work has been to determine when we first began to define "hamburger" as a sandwich distinct from the very similarly prepared entrée served on a plate called a "Hamburg steak." To confuse matters further, at least according to an 1883 *New York Sun* article, some folks in New York City decided to call Hamburg steaks "Hamburgers."[20]

See how easy it is to get confused. One can't simply assume the language of today is the same as the language of yesterday. You must dig down deep into a story and read it within the context of other newspaper articles of that era. Short of this, the novice researcher can be tricked into making false conclusions.

For example, the 1883 article begins with the sentence "'Give me six Hamburgers, four chops, half a pound of sliced ham, and five cents' worth of pickles,' said a bareheaded girl, as she entered a small store that stands near a towering cigar factory on Second avenue." In today's language, it sounds like she's ordering fast food burgers – sandwiches – in addition to the usual deli fare. You might think this, but you'd be wrong.

The reporter includes this line that clearly states what the lunch counter is selling are not sandwiches "Those flat, brown meat cakes on that dish there are Hamburg steaks; the people call them 'Hamburgers.'"

While the article references "pork chops, which are nicely cooked, and weigh at least quarter of a pound. One of them, with some bread, makes a fair meal," it does not imply such a thing as a "pork chop sandwich" and plainly does not link the bread to the Hamburg steak. In fact, to make it clear the article is not referring to anything resembling a "Hamburg sandwich," it states of the meat the girl ordered: "A nice meat lunch for 5 or 10 cents is an attraction, and is better than bringing a sandwich in one's pocket." Finally, the closing paragraph does refer to ham and Swiss sandwiches as a separate item that the girl did not buy.

This is just one example of the confusion concerning the origin of the hamburger. Further muddling matters are the many recipes for "Hamburg steaks" that dotted both books and newspapers. For example, we mentioned the 1885 recipe for Hamburg steak that first appeared in the *Philadelphia Caterer*. Similar recipes appear earlier in other papers and in several cook books, (including, ironically, the 1891 cookbook referenced by John C. Kunzog in his book *Tanbark and Tinsel* where the Menches brothers/Erie County Fair hamburger origin is detailed).

All these recipes reference "Hamburg steak," which is served on a plate with gravy, sometimes with bread, but not in sandwich form. "Hamburg steak" (a.k.a. "Salisbury steak" and "Hamburger steak") would not have been considered a "hamburger" sandwich by any contemporaries of the 1880s and 1890s. In fact, the closest we get to a hamburger sandwich is an 1881 article referencing a "chopped beef" breakfast sandwich prepared for the dying President Garfield as part of his medicinal diet.[21] (As cook books of the era state,[22] chopped beef – served raw or cooked, including in the form of Hamburg Steaks – were recommended for diets of sick people because it is easier for the stomach to digest.)

On the subject of cookbooks, we can use them only as a means of distinguishing recipes. We cannot use them as evidence that a particular recipe was actually a product sold at that time. That would be like saying Groucho Marx actually did shoot an elephant in his pajamas simply because it was written in the script of *Animal Crackers*. No, what we're seeking is the best evidence pointing to, (or in the case of "eliminate the impossible," away from), the most likely suspect.

With the help of Sherlock Holmes, we have dispatched with two of our suspects – the St. Louis World's Fair and Louis' Lunch. But we've gone as far as Sir Arthur Conan Doyle's creation can take us. Next, we'll apply tracking techniques of the Old West in...

The Texas Two Step

CHAPTER TWELVE:
THE TEXAS TWO-STEP

"He answered, like a wave on a rock, who in this land appears like me? Heroes stand not in my presence: they fall to earth beneath my hand. None can meet Swaran in the fight but Fingal, king of stormy hills. Once we wrestled on the heath of Malmor, and our heels overturned the wood. Rocks fell from their place; and rivulets, changing their course, fled murmuring from our strife."

From *FINGAL, An Ancient Epic Poem. In Six Books, Together with Several other Poems, composed by OSSIAN the Son of FINGAL,* Translated from the Gallic Language, By James MacPherson. (Published by Richard Fitzsimons, Dublin, 1762)

Scottish poet James MacPherson stunned the literary world when he published an English translation of the epic Gaelic poems of Ossian, son of Fingal. MacPherson had discovered the original Gaelic verse from this ancient Celtic bard, whose eloquence rivaled Homer. Indeed Ossian – and MacPherson – instantly found international fame. Napoleon, Diderot, and Voltaire all appreciated the work. Thomas Jefferson said of Ossian "I am not ashamed to own that I think this rude bard of the North the greatest Poet that has ever existed" and vowed to learn Gaelic just so he could read Ossian in the original.[1]

Ossian's influence continued well into the nineteenth century, inspiring composers like Felix Mendelson, artists like Jean-Auguste-Dominique Ingres, and poets like William Wordsworth. Yet, the Ossian works were met with controversy from the moment they were first published. It seemed the Irish laid claim to their Celtic origins, and would have none of MacPherson's Scottish origin story. Fortunately, the writing itself provided clues that good literary trackers could use to prove Ossian's actual heritage.

Think of this "tracking" the same way an old west posse might track a fleeing horse thief. Every story leaves a set of literary hoofprints any good scout can follow. This is the technique we'll use as we analyze the three hamburger origin stories that remain standing.

In the last chapter we left off with three lingering suspects in our search for who sold the first hamburger: Fletcher Davis of Athens, Texas (in the late 1880s), Charles Nagreen from Seymour, Wisconsin (1885), and the Menches Brothers (Charles and Frank, 1885). Each has their own story. We'll apply a form of modern forensic analysis to see if we can dig up corroborating evidence from independent contemporary sources.

Let's start with Fletcher Davis. Others have already provided most of the legwork here, so I will merely summarize. First, Fletcher Davis is reputed to be the "unknown food vender" interviewed for the *New York Tribune* story about the hamburger's invention at the 1904 St. Louis World's Fair. The reporter is quoted as writing the popular sandwich was "the innovation of a food vendor on the pike." This was the story "painstakingly" researched and reported by *Dallas Morning News* columnist Frank X. Tolbert from 1974-1976 at the prompting of Clint Murchison, Jr., then owner of the Dallas Cowboys.

Murchison was upset by the *New York Times* story highlighting Louis' Lunch claim to have been the first joint to serve a burger. Tolbert wrote that the incensed Murchison said, "If we let the Yankees get away with claiming the invention of the hamburgers, they'll be going after chili con carne next."[2]

Now, that *New York Times* story offered the Cowboys' owner a hole big enough to run through, and run he did, as lead blocker for the investigating reporter Tolbert. The *Times* wrote of the Louis' Lunch claim, "The only other serious challenge to the title is a theory supported by the McDonald's Corporation, the giant nationwide hamburger chain. Historians at McDonald's Hamburger University have researched the problem, the company says, and claim the inventor was an unknown food vender at the St. Louis Fair of 1904."[3] This qualification provided Tolbert the opening he needed.

In his initial column on the topic, Frank Tolbert quotes Murchison saying Fletcher Davis' sandwich "became so appreciated locally that the Athens Chamber of Commerce got together a kitty and sent Dave to the 1904 World's Fair in St. Louis to advertise the city. A fancy dan reporter from the old *New York Tribune* interviewed Dave about his hamburger."[4]

In terms of "tracking," there's no bigger hoofprint than a reference to an article in a major metropolitan newspaper. More so when we have a direct quote from that article.

There's only one problem. No such *New York Tribune* story exists. I searched the complete digitized records of the *New York Tribune* and found nothing. It turns out I'm not the first to do this. Josh Ozersky wrote "My research assistant, Andrea Murphy, and I have painstakingly looked through the *Tribune's* archives and can safely say that this report does not exist."[5]

This isn't corroborating evidence. It's quite the opposite. In fact, the first reference to a "*New York Tribune* article" appears to be Murchison's quote in that very first column Tolbert wrote.

Things get worse for "Old Dave" and Tolbert's assertion that he was the "unknown vendor on the pike." Historian Pamela J. Vaccaro in her book *Beyond The Ice Cream Cone - The Whole Scoop on Food at the 1904 World's Fair*, says "There is no Fletcher Davis on the official concessionaire's list or on the final financial balance sheet of the LPE Co., and the company certainly would not have let anyone exert any kind of 'squatter's rights.'"[6]

Sounds pretty bad, right? It turns out some of Fletch's kinfolk remember going to the 1904 St. Louis World's Fair and seeing Old Dave there. They even showed Gary Cartwright, a writer for *Texas Monthly*, the vendor ticket stubs Fletch used to get into the St. Louis event. So much for the veracity of those "vendor's lists."

But wait a minute. Upon further review, Cartwright "saw that the vendor's tickets issued to Fletcher Davis identified him as 'a pottery turner' representing W. S. Ceramics Co. at the fair's Palace of Mines and Metallurgy."[7]

None of this helps Davis' case. Worse, Cartwright reports the family says the earliest newspaper account of him cooking hamburgers didn't appear until at least 1896 and it's likely he didn't even move to Athens until 1894.[8] This 1894 date is consistent with what we learned in Chapter 7. Fletcher's first wife died in Illinois in 1892, so it's unlikely he would have been to Athens before then. He married his second wife in Athens in 1896, so that might account for his name appearing in the local newspaper at that time. Finally, his 1940 obituary said he first came to Athens "45 years ago" (1895) and "returned to Illinois for a short time and then came back to this county where he had since made his home."[9]

Rather than corroborating, most of what we've seen comes closer to refuting the Davis claim. Worse, Kent Biffle wrote in the *Dallas Morning News* that the Davis theory "isn't helped by the reputations of Mr. Tolbert and Mr. Murchison as notorious pranksters. Mr. Tolbert would order an unwanted load of fertilizer dumped on one's front yard. Mr. Murchison would move one's 40 foot-yacht into one's 42-foot swimming pool while one was out of town. Things like that."[10]

It also doesn't help that one of Tolbert's columns on the matter appeared on April Fools' Day.[11]

I don't know if this is enough to fully eliminate Davis. If, however, he did start cooking hamburgers in 1896, or even 1894, as has been pointed out previously, there's plenty of evidence that folks were already gaga over hamburgers. That means he likely wasn't the first to sell a hamburger.

Who knows, maybe Clint Jr.'s grandfather ate those hamburgers before Clint Sr. was born (in 1895) in a different place. Perhaps he traveled slightly south of Athens, between San Antonio and Houston, to Moulton, Texas. There, in 1894, Barny's saloon served up "hamburger steak sandwiches every day of the week." Or so tells the bar's advertisement, that ran from April through September of that year.[12]

All this probably won't persuade the citizens of Athens, Texas to alter their festivities. As the mayor of Athens once said when confronted with Oklahoma's Oscar Weber Bilby's story, "We don't think it's going to take away from us. We're Texans – we reserve all bragging rights."[13]

Oh, and, by the way, the Poems of Ossian turned out to be one of literary history's greatest hoaxes. Nonetheless, it remains in print and is still taught in college level literature classes. So much for the idea that fake news is a recent phenomenon.

Speaking of fake news, did you ever wonder how easy it is to make? The next chapter shows you point-by-point one example of how it is done. If you're paying close attention, it just might remind you of one of your favorite childhood games. What's more, have you ever had to convince someone to buy something from you? You'll definitely want to turn the page to find out why…

IT'S THE SIZZLE THAT SELLS, NOT THE STEAK

CHAPTER THIRTEEN:
IT'S THE SIZZLE THAT SELLS, NOT THE STEAK

We all know the story by now. Fletcher Davis, a part-time lunch counter cook at J. J. Powers Drug Store and a potter by trade, invented the hamburger in Athens, Texas sometime in the 1880s or 1890s. So impressed were the kind citizens of that small town that the Chamber of Commerce collected money to send "Old Dave" off to the 1904 St. Louis World's Fair where he wowed the international crowd with his culinary invention. Fletch's unnamed sandwich earned the name "Hamburger" courtesy of St. Louis' German immigrants. It caught the interest of a reporter from the *New York Tribune* who wrote the story proclaiming this new food sensation "was the idea of a food purveyor on the pike."

Although the reporter left the name of that food vendor out, in 1976, "after two years of sweat-neck research," *Dallas Morning News* Columnist Frank X. Tolbert determined that unknown vendor was non-other than Athens' own Fletcher Davis. Bolstering Tolbert's claim was a report that historians from the much-esteemed McDonald's Hamburger University confirmed the *New York Tribune* story.

By the time Tolbert published this story in his 1983 book *Tolbert's Texas*, the myth of Fletcher Davis and the St. Louis World's Fair had taken off. Despite competing claims, it rose ascendant. A 2004 Associated Press report under the banner "Burger's Birthday," stated, "There are at least four claims to creating the first hamburger sandwich, all with their merits and weaknesses, but the moment that the hamburger garnered national attention is generally accepted as being in 1904 at the St. Louis World's Fair – hence the 100th birthday. That's where Davis Fletcher (sic) of Austin, Texas, served his version and received glowing reviews from newspapers as far away as New York."[1]

Thanks to the work of writers like Kent Biffle, Josh Ozersky, Gary Cartwright, and Pamela J. Vaccaro, we now know the story of Fletcher

Davis, specifically, and of the St. Louis World's Fair generally, to be false. The more curious of us ask, "How could such an obviously false story – a.k.a. "fake news" to use the now popular expression – have come about in the first place.

To discover the source of this faux hamburger origin story, I decided to reverse engineer the paper trail – literally, the "newspaper" trail. Starting with the 2004 AP story, which, being AP, probably was picked up in a number of papers, let's work backwards to see what we can piece together.

"Historians have long agreed that the first hamburger sandwich was introduced by an 'unknown purveyor' at the 1904 St. Louis World's Fair," read the flyer for Frank X Tolbert's 1979 hamburger cook-off. Celebrating the 75th anniversary of the hamburger's "birth" at the St. Louis World's Fair, that cook-off became a major story. Over a span of two months that summer, the story – and that line "Historians have long agreed…" appeared in at least two dozen newspapers from Hawaii to Quebec.[2] From that point until Vaccaro's 2004 book *Beyond The Ice Cream Cone - The Whole Scoop on Food at the 1904 World's Fair* first hinted a credibility problem existed in the Fletcher Davis account through the St. Louis story's final nail in the coffin courtesy of Ozersky's damning 2007 article in the *Los Angeles Times*,[3] the St. Louis World's Fair hamburger origin story represented the classic file story every media outlet possessed.

It's clear that this 1979 story came about due to the 75th anniversary celebration of the St. Louis World's Fair. The "fact checked" support for this 1979 story was Tolbert's 1976 column (and, indeed, all five of Tolbert's columns on this topic dating back from 1974).

Prior to this, much of the 1970s represented a tug-of-war between the Fletcher Davis/St. Louis World's Fair and Louis' Lunch origin stories. Wire stories coming out of the *Chicago Tribune*[4] and the *New York Times*[5] trumpeted this rivalry.

In December 1974, several Texas papers printed the Jack Maguire "Talk of Texas" column.[6] Maguire echoed Tolbert's columns from earlier that year. Maguire mimicked most of Tolbert, although he mistakenly references the old article as from the "*New York Herald-*

Tribune," not the "*New York Tribune*" cited by Tolbert. For the record, the *New York Tribune* acquired the *New York Herald* in 1924, two decades after the St. Louis World's Fair. The combined paper initially published under the banner "*New York Herald and New York Tribune*" until shortening it to the simplified *New York Herald-Tribune* in 1926.

Tolbert's February 3, 1974 column was the first reference to the *New York Tribune*, although the actual quote attributed to the *New York Tribune* – "the idea of a food purveyor on the pike" – didn't first appear until Tolbert's July 18, 1976 column. Of note, in the chapter of his book *Tolbert's Texas*, the quote was changed to "the *innovation* of a food *vendor* on the pike."

Throughout 1974, at least a half dozen papers[7] picked up another wire story from the *Chicago Tribune*[8]. This story originated prior to Tolbert's initial column and merely referenced the St. Louis World's Fair hamburger origin story without mentioning an "Old Dave," Athens, Texas, the *New York Tribune*, or even McDonald's Hamburger University.

The first definitive mention of McDonald's and the St. Louis Fair was in the January 1974 *New York Times* story about Louis' Lunch (as mentioned in the previous chapter). Recall the quote: "Historians at McDonald's Hamburger University have researched the problem, the company says, and claim the inventor was an unknown food vender at the St. Louis Fair of 1904."[9]

That statement is not sourced and it's difficult to fact check where it came from. A reference to the hamburger being "introduced to the rest of the U.S. at the St. Louis World's Fair in 1904" did appear in a footnote to a cover story on McDonald's in *Time Magazine* a few months prior to the *New York Times* article.[10] When asked about the reference in this *New York Times* article, Mike Bullington, Archivist at McDonald's Corporation replied, "I have researched our records and I am not able to locate the Hamburger University study."[11]

It's very possible "historians at McDonald's Hamburger University" made no such claim. According to the McDonald's website, Hamburger University was opened in 1961. In 1965, UPI reported McDonald's Vice President James Schindler traveled to Hamburg, Germany to present its mayor "with a plaque to honor the hamburger." Under various headlines, versions of this article appeared in no fewer than thirteen newspapers.[11] The article concluded with "Schindler said German emigrants took their version of the hamburger early in the 19th century to Cincinnati – but the real birth of the hamburger as Americans know it today took place at the 1904 St. Louis World's Fair when an enterprising gent began selling hot hamburgers in a bun."

In fact, if we are to believe John F. Love, author of the 1995 business biography *McDonald's: Behind the Arches*, McDonald's had a reason to refute the St. Louis claim. Love reveals the company's public relations firm purposely promoted provocative origin stories. Love wrote: "McDonald's got free publicity simply by tracing the origin of the hamburger to a period, before its popularly accepted genesis – the St. Louis World's Exposition in 1904."[12] The 1965 Hamburg, Germany PR stunt was one example of this campaign.

It's clear that, at least in 1965, based on Schindler's statement and Love's revelation, "historians at McDonald's Hamburger University" had not yet come to the conclusion that the hamburger's "inventor was an unknown food vender at the St. Louis Fair of 1904."

Neal O'Hara, on the other hand, seems to be quite sure who this vendor was. He wrote in 1955, "The hamburger, as we Americans know it, was invented by e'se(?) Aloysius P. Burns, a concessionaire at the St. Louis World's Fair in 1905 and is therefore celebrating its semi-centennial."[13] Unfortunately, the source of Mr. Burns identity was not revealed and the paper itself was damaged so that portions (right before the name) are illegible. Also, O'Hara got the year of the St. Louis World's Fair wrong. It didn't occur in 1905. It took place in 1904. But, as we shall see, his idea of celebrating its "anniversary" hit the mark with newspaper editors and other astute marketers.

Throughout the early 1950s, newspapers ran "filler facts" (odd trivia meant to fill excess white space on the page) like this: "Hamburgers cooked as we know them today started their rise to fame back in 1904 at the St. Louis World's fair."[14] It was clear the 1904 St. Louis World's Fair hamburger origin myth had been firmly implanted in the public conscious by this time.

But, when was the very first mention of the St. Louis World's Fair and the creation of the hamburger?

Unlike the ice cream cone connection to the 1904 St. Louis World's Fair, whose mention appeared within months after the Exposition closed,[15] it apparently took a good 45 years for the hamburger connection to the St. Louis Fair to emerge.

Dan O'Connell loved hamburgers. In 1928, he relocated his restaurant from Milwaukee to Chicago. His slogan: "Hamburger with onion and pickle for only a nickle (sic)." By 1949 he had expanded his chain to 13 restaurants, all in the Chicago area. He came up with a promotional scheme. He would create "the world's biggest hamburger" and invite anyone named Hamburger to come to his flagship restaurant and have a bite at no cost. To justify the event, he tied it to the anniversary of the 1904 St. Louis World's Fair. A reporter covering this story wrote "His research on the hamburger, O'Connell claims, proves it was merely a dish of shredded raw beef in the German City of Hamburg. Its American start to fame, he contends, began when it was introduced cooked at the St. Louis World's fair in 1904." This was the very first mention of the hamburger being invented at the 1904 St. Louis World's Fair.[16]

Of greater interest is this. The Lubbock story was an INS wire service story (why else would a Texas newspaper pick up a Chicago story?). Another wire service, however, sent out its own version of the same story. It started out this way: "Mark the forty-fifth anniversary of the 'invention' of the hamburger, by some unknown but ingenious chef at the St. Louis World's fair."[17] But don't let the fact this quote came from an article in *The Daily Oklahoman* trick you. This was, in fact, a syndicated story from the *Chicago Tribune* Press Service.

Within two weeks the AP sent out a story covering the aftermath of O'Connell's promotional stunt. That article, picked up by more than half a dozen newspapers, contained this quote: "An unknown chef created the modern hamburger when he broiled ground beef and served it on a bun."[18]

Now, let's repeat the popular lore as it came to be known by the late 1970s. In 1974, after his son informed him of the *New York Times* article on Louis' Lunch, Clint Murchison, Jr. contacted Frank Tolbert. Murchison said "Old Dave" from Athens was the "unknown vendor" at the 1904 St. Louis World's Fair responsible for inventing the hamburger. Furthermore, Murchison remembers the source of this fact as an article from the *New York Tribune*.

Could it be Murchison misremembered the source? Is it possible he read it in a Texas newspaper that picked up the *Chicago Tribune* Press Service story? Heck, we know an Oklahoma paper did, so why not a Texas paper?

It's amazing how one wildly successful (in terms of publicity, at least) promotional idea can be responsible for an elaborate and enduring – albeit totally false – myth.

It's like the "telephone game." You know that popular icebreaker played at parties and other group gatherings. You put people in a line and the first person whispers a quick story to the person next to them. Each recipient then turns to the next person and repeats the story, or at least as much of the story that can be remembered. By the end of the line, the story has taken on a life of its own.

That appears to describe how the St. Louis World's Fair hamburger origin myth blossomed from an embellished press release to a newspaper "fact filler" to a major investigative report to a newspaper file story (under the category "settled science") that everyone assumed to be true.

Now you have a better idea on how that happened.

Along the way, you've probably also discovered why it's the sizzle that sells, not the steak.

And then there were two.

Next we'll take a look at Charles "Hamburger Charlie" Nagreen's story. We'll tell you right off the bat, as far as we can tell, of all the claimants, he sold hamburgers for the longest time. But was he the first? Find out what the research reveals in…

A (Swiss) Cheesehead Tale

ACT THREE:

– THE REVEAL –

FORENSIC ANALYSIS

CHAPTER FOURTEEN:
A (SWISS) CHEESEHEAD TALE

"Memories don't just fade, as the old saying would have us believe; they also grow. What fades is the initial perception, the actual experience of the events. But every time we recall an event, we must reconstruct the memory, and with each recollection the memory may be changed – colored by succeeding events, other people's recollections or suggestions, increased understanding, or a new context."

From *Witness For the Defense: The Accused, the Eyewitness, and the Expert Who Puts Memory On Trial*, by Dr. Elizabeth Loftus and Katherine Ketcham (St. Martin's Press, 1991)

When you're a reporter, you often find yourself interviewing sources to try to get a broader perspective on the story. Reporters will often quote the source directly. If the source offers a fact that may be controversial, a good reporter will try to obtain the same information from a second, independent source. This represents a form of fact checking you might call "Journalism 101."

Police investigators and trial attorneys face similar challenges when interviewing witnesses. They realize memory can play tricks. As time goes by, memories can develop holes. Dr. Samuel "Sam" Beckett in the TV series *Quantum Leap* described this phenomenon as the "Swiss cheese effect." Once these holes develop, it's easy to fill them in with anything that sounds reasonable. Indeed, there have been cases where investigators and prosecutors, by using a certain sequence of questions, have placed false memories within the minds of the witnesses they are questioning.[1]

To overcome this challenge, like the journalist, legal analysts will seek a second, independent witness to provide corroborating evidence. But what happens when that second witness does not exist? Then the investigator must search for other forms of corroborating evidence.

That's our mission in the next three episodes of our "Hamburger WhoDunit" serial.

Let's start by tackling the story of Charles Nagreen, a.k.a., "Hamburger Charlie," as he's known by the friendly folks in Wisconsin. This shouldn't be confused with "Hamburger Charlie," the proprietor of the World Lunch Room, located at 165 South Commercial Street in Salem, Oregon, who placed a want ad in 1909 seeking "500 men to dirty dishes for two dishwashers."[2]

The "Hamburger Charlie" we're talking about here, as near as we can tell, first appeared in the newspapers 10 years later proudly advertising the fact that he "will serve refreshments at the big picnic at Binghamton Sunday, June 15th."[3]

Hamburger Charlie (again, or "Hamburger Charley," as newspapers refer to Nagreen both ways) began selling hamburgers at the age of 15 when he took his horse-drawn cart 20+ miles from his home in Hortonsville to the first Seymour Fair. Immediately after, he went to the New London Fair, only to be turned away. He then proceeded to the Oshkosh Fair, but lost the $30 he earned in Seymour along the way. He borrowed $10 and entered the Oshkosh Fair upon the invitation of Ira Parker, president of the Oshkosh fair, who reportedly said, "come in, set up your stand, and do business." On his way back home, an unknown farmer returned the lost $30 to Charlie.[4]

This was the story told 49 years after the fact in 1934. Charlie was interviewed by *The Post Crescent*, the local newspaper that covered his town[5]. It is the first recorded telling of the story as far as research has been able to identify. Oddly, that article didn't mention anything about him making hamburgers. Within a week of publication, 81-year-old James Christensen wrote back to the paper saying he was the unknown farmer.[6]

Now that's corroboration. In this subsequent story, we finally see this quick sentence, "Mr. Nagreen launched his first hamburger stand at the Seymour fair in 1885."[7]

Thanks to James Christensen, it appears we have an independent second source to confirm Hamburger Charlie's story – at least about losing the $30.

As with all these stories, there's no contemporary "smoking gun." There's no newspaper article saying, "so-and-so invented the hamburger at this year's fair." All we can do is piece together circumstantial evidence that supports the story.

Charley gave us a few more facts we can double check. And, since all good reporters don't want to be accused of "fake news," we double check the facts we have. In this case, we have Charley's statement that he attended "the first Seymour Fair" and then attended the Oshkosh Fair after being rejected from the New London Fair. So we have a specific event (the "first" Seymour Fair) and a sequence of subsequent events (the other fairs). We also have access to contemporary newspaper articles to verify these facts. Here's what we found out.

The "first" Seymour Fair in fact did occur in 1885.[8] Score another corroboration point for Charlie. As long as the New London Fair followed immediately, and the Oshkosh Fair followed after that, then Hamburger Charlie is in the clear.

This is where the problems begin. The Seymour Fair was October 6th, 7th, and 8th. The Oshkosh Fair was almost a month earlier.[9] And there was no New London Fair that year. In fact, New London didn't hold its first fair until September 18th, 1891.[10]

Looks like we found a hole in Charles Nagreen's story. Just for fun, let's check the 1891 dates of the Seymour Fair and Oshkosh Fair. It turns out the Seymour Fair occurred immediately before the New London Fair in 1891.[11] Furthermore, the Oshkosh Fair took place right after the New London Fair.[12] So, maybe Charlie lost his $30 in 1891, not 1885.

It gets worse still. The 1934 retelling of Charles Nagreen's hamburger origin story claims Ira Parker, president of the Oshkosh Fair, invited the young Hamburger Charlie to set up his stand. This would have been quite a feat for Ira in either 1885 or 1891. Ira Parker was living in Chicago at this time. He didn't move to Oshkosh until 1896. Furthermore, according to his 1934 obituary, he "had been connected with the Winnebago County Fair association, as a director, for 24 years, and he held the office of superintendent of privileges each year during the fall exposition."[13] This means his affiliation with the fair began in 1910.

The 1891 sequence matches the oft-repeated Charles Nagreen story. Does this mean he actually invented the hamburger in 1891? Or does it simply mean he lost his $30 in 1891? We can't tell for sure. What we do know is that our corroborating evidence more likely addresses the lost $30 story than the hamburger creation story. And where does Ira Parker really fit into this? In the end, we're left with nothing to corroborate the idea that Hamburger Charlie first put his flattened meatballs between two slices of bread at the Seymour Fair on October 6th, 7th, or 8th in 1885. The entire story, for all we know, may have simply been an exaggeration for the benefit of local readers (and customers). After all, as we learned in Chapter 4, Charlie Nagreen was the consummate carnival barker. He knew a thing or two about storytelling, smart marketing, and, more importantly, self-promotion.

But what about the Menches Brothers? Did they also encourage local reporters to exaggerate their tale? They certainly had a business motivation to do so. This might explain why newspaper accounts detail multiple – and conflicting – versions of their claim to have invented the hamburger. And if their 1885 story holds up, did it occur before the Seymour Fair in Outagamie Wisconsin? We'll visit the first of the competing stories from our final contender on our trek to determine which story is most likely the real story next in…

Marketing 101: Know Your Audience

CHAPTER TEN:
MARKETING 101: KNOW YOUR AUDIENCE

And then there was one. Or two. Or three.

The Menches brothers' hamburger origin story appears to have evolved over time. It's easy to see how the Menches' meandering story harms their credibility as contenders in the mystery of who sold the first hamburger. This isn't necessarily their fault. An enthusiastic local press might have had a hand in this.

The first story appeared in print in 1922. Of note, this is also the earliest documented hamburger origin story. In this version, the reporter offers very few direct quotes. A single quote addresses the hamburger. In his article, the reporter attributes Charles Menches with saying, "We sell a ton of chopped beef or hamburger in sandwiches, and a pound will make on an average, 15 sandwiches. We have been selling hamburger sandwiches for 20 years."[1]

From a historical perspective and based on what we now know from Chapter 10, it's interesting to note how the reporter phrases Charles' terminology for the product. It's referred to as both "hamburger in sandwiches" and "hamburger sandwiches." At this point in hamburger history, White Castle was only a year old and was just beginning to expand outside its hometown of Wichita, Kansas.

It's hard to determine if the one direct quote from Charles in this 1922 article is actual or paraphrased by the reporter because the article contains obvious factual errors. For example, the article references the Menches creation of the ice cream cone to the 1893 Chicago World's Fair, when we know the event is more accurately associated with the 1904 St. Louis World's Fair. Based on the timeline offered in the article, the reporter has the Menches Brothers making waffle cones in Akron about five years before they actually moved to Akron.

In addition, the report seems to interchange the terms "hot dog" and "hamburger" as if they refer to the same sandwich. The piece implies the hamburger sandwich morphed from the hot dog, with the customers telling the Menches brothers to switch from a mixed pork and beef product to a beef-only product. This statement was not attributed to Charles and was never again cited as the reason why the Menches Brothers came up with the idea for the hamburger sandwich.

The article then says, "For the last 40 years they have sold 'hot dog' sandwich at Summit county fairs." Other reports and interviews state the Menches Brothers first served the Summit County Fair in 1884,[2] which is roughly 40 years (actually 38) prior to the year this article was written. So, which is it? 20 years (1902)? Or 40 years (1882)?

And, if, as the article says, the Menches Brothers had been selling "hot dogs" for the last 40 years, why does a 1906 picture of one of the Menches Brothers' concessionaire tent list only "Hot Sausage" and "Hot Hambergs" (sic)? Could the article have meant "hot sausage" instead of "hot dog"? (This may explain why "hot dog" always appears in quotes in the article.) Also, notice what they were calling (albeit misspelled) the hamburger sandwich almost two decades prior to when this reporter penned the article.

This 1922 articles contains too many factual errors and historical inconsistencies to be taken seriously. Is this Charles' fault? At the time of the interview, Charles was 63 years old. Though still relatively young, could his memory have begun to play tricks on him? Or was Charles using the publicity to promote his local businesses by giving his audience a feeling of cause célèbre?

On the other hand, was the reporter too willing to write the story without at least a modest amount of fact checking? And why wasn't Frank Menches included? He was certainly around then. The article contains too many questions to be considered credible.

More than 15 years later, we finally get to hear Frank's "local" version of the Menches hamburger origin story. This time there would be specific facts that would allow us to dissect the various components of the story. As a backdrop, recall that, by 1938, Wimpy's "I'll gladly pay you Tuesday for a hamburger today" had already catapulted the cartoon character into pop culture history. In addition, s few years earlier the rapidly growing White Castle had relocated its headquarters to Columbus, Ohio, Akron's intrastate rival.

While the 1922 article couldn't decide if the Menches started in 1882 or 1902, in 1938 columnist H. B. (Doc) Kerr, decided to split the difference. His column says, "The hamburger sandwich was born on the old Summit county fairgrounds here in the fall of 1892."[3] In the piece, Kerr appears to be telling Frank Menches' story. He even includes several quotes. Again, it's difficult to determine if these are actual quotes or paraphrases.

In a nutshell, here's the story reported by Kerr: The Menches Brothers run out of pork and called Zimmerly Brothers, a local packer, to order more. The "linker" had gone off duty, so Zimmerly Brothers said they couldn't fill the order. Frank recalls, at the time, "we were paying 12 cents a pound for sausage. Beef was selling at 8 cents a pound." He talked it over with Charles and they decided to get ground beef from Al Boder's butcher shop on 115 N. Howard Street.

Here's the problem with this story. Zimmerly Brothers didn't open for business until 1894 – two years after the alleged 1892 invention of the hamburger.[4] Furthermore, the wholesale price of beef in 1892 was 6 cents, although the price of sausage, at 12½ cents, was closer to what Frank said it was.[5] On the positive side, Al Boder was advertising hams for 10 cents a pound in 1892 from his shop on 115 N. Howard St., so we know he was around.[6] In fact, Al wouldn't move his butcher shop until 1914.[7]

That means Zimmerly Brothers and Al Boder were both in business in 1902. Could it be that, despite the very poor reporting in the 1922 article, Charles' original origin story was correct? Was it possible Frank's meat prices were a better fit for 1902? Likely not. Dressed beef was in the high end of the range (7-10 ½ cents per pound). Sausage was also probably too high as comparable pork products (i.e., sugar cured ham) were 3-4 cents more expensive in 1902 compared to 1892 (when sausage was in the range at 12½ cents per pound).[8]

If the numbers didn't make sense, how did the Menches brothers Akron origin story get printed in the first place. Perhaps "story" is more appropriate here than you imagine. The columnist who wrote Frank's story – Doc Kerr – published several columns on the Menches Brothers during a short span of time in the last month of 1938. He described Frank as someone who "is blessed with a good memory and can tell many entertaining tales of his life."[9]

Certainly, as explained in Chapter 8, the Menches brothers had a business motive to promote an Akron-centered version of their involvement in the birth of the hamburger. It's possible the local press had their own motives (beyond showing up Columbus, Ohio).

Zimmerly Brothers figured prominently in Frank's 1938 retelling of the Menches story. It turns out Zimmerly Brothers was a major advertiser in *The Akron Beacon Journal* (the paper that printed the story). They had been since the early 1900s, although in the first couple of decades they shifted their advertising back and forth between competing newspapers before settling back again with the *Beacon Journal*. Doc Kerr may not have deliberately inserted Zimmerly Brothers into the 1892 tale, but the paper's publisher was no doubt pleased to see his big customer mentioned.

Despite these apparent conflicts in this story, it was repeated again and again in the *Beacon Journal*. A year after Frank's version was published, the *Beacon Journal* merged the brothers' two earlier published accounts into a single hybrid piece that returned the origin year to 1902.[10] A decade later a new columnist in the same paper essentially rehashed the Doc Kerr's columns into a single column, again using the 1892 date as the year of origin.[11] This time 1892 stuck. So pervasive was this story that the Associated Press included it in Frank's obituary in 1951.[12]

It's very possible both Charles and Frank, no doubt familiar with the art of showmanship, were playing to the local audience. The local media might have been all too obliging.

But that wasn't the only story the boys told. In fact, it's very possible the very first hamburger origin story they told was the actual truth. Why might we say this? Because it was told without the understanding it would be published and in a manner that certainly didn't appeal to the journalist's home town bias. What's more this particular story contains many more facts. The more facts you have, the easier it is to prove – or disprove – a story.

And speaking of facts, here's one to chew on. Frank told Doc Kerr in his 1938 interview "As I recall, we were paying 12 cents a pound for sausage. Beef was selling at 8 cents a pound." We now know those prices don't agree with the prices in either 1892 or 1902. Oddly enough, in 1885, the pricing does match – the price of pork sausage was 12½ cents per pound and the price of beef was 6-8 cents per pound.[13]

Coincidence?

Perhaps.

Perhaps not.

In either case, remember this as we enter our Hamburger WhoDunIt's most rigorous analysis yet in…

CSI: Hamburg(er), N.Y.

CHAPTER SIXTEEN:
CSI: HAMBURG(ER), N.Y.

"Some circumstantial evidence is very strong, as when you find a trout in the milk."

– Henry David Thoreau

C harles and Frank Menches were born in Canton, Ohio. Their father, Jacob Menches, an engineer in Prussia, immigrated to America and became a grocer in Canton. Their mother, Charlotte Hahn Menches, was originally from France. As young men, both boys were quite athletic. Charles was a well-regarded gymnast who travelled with a popular circus as a trapeze artist and high wire walker before he turned twenty.[1] Frank, six years younger than Charles, was an award-winning bicycle racer.[2,3]

While the brothers' lives contain several amazing stories (which we explored in Chapter 3), our focus here is on only one: Their role as (potentially) the first to sell a hamburg sandwich. How this story became known is itself a story. The brothers' claim was widely acknowledged (the headline of Frank's 1951 obituary reads "'Inventor' of Hamburger Dies"[4]). The real story, however, lay hidden for half a century and was published decades after the brothers had passed away.

Born in Jamestown, New York, John C. Kunzog worked in the newspaper business his entire career. During his lifetime, he was regarded as an expert on circus history in America. In 1962, he published his first book, *The One Horse Show—The Life and Times of Dan Rice, Circus Jester and Philanthropist*. Kunzog's interest in Dan Rice developed while running a weekly community newspaper in Hudson, Ohio. His salesman, "an elderly man by the name of William M. (Pop) Robinson" entertained the twenty-eight-year-old Kunzog with stories of his circus tour with Dan Rice in 1864.[5]

That wasn't the only story Pop told Kunzog. In 1970, Kunzog published his second book, *Tanbark and Tinsel – A Galaxy of Glittering*

Gems from the Dazzling Diadem of Circus History. There, on page 155, Kunzog mentions that, during his tenure in Hudson, "I employed as salesman an elderly man who had a circus background, and when he learned I had written publicity for circuses, he regaled me with stories of the past." No doubt that "elderly man" was Pop, and Pop's stories included that of Frank and Charles Menches.

By then, the Menches brothers were nearing retirement and had reduced their once thriving concession business to focus on other business ventures. They had recently sold the assets of their Premium Candy, Corn and Cone Company. This company produced, among other things, Gee-Whiz caramel corn (a contemporary rival of the Crackerjacks brand), and the ubiquitous Waffle Cone.[6] In 1917, they used the proceeds from that sale to build what would eventually become the Liberty Theater, which they remodeled handsomely in 1921.[7]

In his 1970 book, Kunzog says he met with Frank Menches in the early 1920s. This is believable because contemporary newspaper accounts confirm Kunzog published the Hudson newspaper at least from 1920 through 1923.[8] The level of detail relayed in *Tanbark and Tinsel* has made this the definitive Menches Brothers hamburger origin story. It also provides many opportunities to corroborate – or refute – the report.

Let's start with the obvious. This is the only hamburger origin story that does not have the subject of the story championing the cause to a local reporter. What's more, Kunzog, unlike the other newspaper writers, was considered by his peers to be a very credible reporter in this subject area. That being said, as we'll soon discover, his retelling of Frank Menches hamburger origin story contains some noticeable errors.

Let's summarize Kunzog by focusing on the salient facts.

First, the set-up: The event occurred at the Erie County (N.Y.) Agricultural Society's Annual Fair (a.k.a., the "Erie County Fair" or the "Hamburg Fair") in Hamburg, N.Y. when Frank was 20 years old. At that time, the women's auxiliary, a particularly vocal group, had asked the society to eliminate wood and coal fueled ovens used by food vendors. It seems the year earlier a renegade ember had landed on a woman's dress causing it to catch fire. In addition to this concern, the

Society had built a new wooden grandstand. The commissioners decided to allow only gas-powered stoves near the grandstand. The Menches Brothers used gas-powered stoves.

And now, the actual day of the event: The brothers run out of pork for their sandwiches. Frank approaches "Andrew Klein," a local butcher. Mr. Klein declines to provide Frank with pork. The weather is too hot and humid, so it doesn't make sense to slaughter an entire pig for the few pounds of meat Frank wanted. Instead, Klein gives Frank a few pounds of ground beef. Not quite sure, the brothers experimented with forming this meat into the same kind of patties they had normally formed from sausage. They added various ingredients to help the cooking process and improve the flavor.

It was a hit! Kunzog writes a satisfied customer approached Frank and asked, "Gutte Schmeck! Vas ist?" ("Good tasting. What is it?") To which, Frank is said to have replied "Hamburger, das allerbeste!" ("the very best!")

Kunzog included far more details, but the ones listed here are the most important. Let's go back to the Wayback Machine (i.e., old newspaper archives) and measure how Kunzog's account scores on the old fact-checking scale.

First, Frank Menches turned twenty on July 16, 1885. The Erie County Fair was held from September 15th through September 18th that year[9]. (This would have been three weeks *before* Charlie Nagreen's hamburger origin story took place.) Frank was indeed twenty by the time of the 1885 Erie County Fair. Score one for Kunzog.

Or not.

Remember, Kunzog is retelling Frank's story half a century after Frank originally told it to him. And Frank told it to him 35 years after the event occurred. So, "20 years old" may be real or it may be a convenient rounding by either Frank or Kunzog. Throwing suspicion on the age is Kunzog's incorrect claim that Charles was sixteen years younger than Frank. In fact, Frank was six years younger than Charles. This is not a mistake Frank would make. It's more likely something got transposed in Kunzog's notes. Could other items have been incorrectly noted?

That's why the other corroborating facts are important. It would be nice if we had a complete list of approved vendors for the 1885 Erie County Fair from a contemporary source. The only such available source merely contains a partial list of vendors.[10] In reviewing the Menches brothers' story one hundred years later, Hamburg Town Historian James Swinnich incorrectly assumed this was a complete list of licensees.[11] We know it's a partial list because newspaper reports of the time reference a variety of food vendors not included on this list (e.g., "Ex-side Justice Read, of the county court, presides over a lemonade and pop stand with dignity and grace" and "The pop and peanut venders are in their glory"[12] as well as "The grounds are thickly dotted with booths where the concoctors of cream candy, ham sandwiches, and diluted lemon juice hold sway"[13]).

Alternatively, it would be nice if we had some record of the whereabouts of the Menches brothers from September 15-18, 1885. We don't. Since we know they started their concession business a year earlier, it's possible they could have been at the 1885 Stark County Fair in their hometown of Canton, Ohio. But that occurred from September 28th through October 2nd,[14] giving the brothers plenty of time to travel back and forth. The Akron (Ohio) Fair was held after the Stark County Fair,[15] so that would not have posed a conflict, either.

Furthermore, interviews with the Menches family indicate Charles and Frank were introduced to the Erie County (N.Y.) Fair through their contacts in Jamestown and Dunkirk.[16] The 1885 Chautauqua County Fair (Jamestown) occurred from September 1-4 and the 1885 Northern Chautauqua Fair (Dunkirk-Fredonia) was held from September 22-26. For that matter, the Cattaraugus County Fair (Olean) was from September 7-10. It would therefore make sense for the Menches brothers to have hit all Western New York fairs in the sequence they were held before returning to their home region and participating in that county fair circuit.

All the above does is prove there's no obvious conflict that would keep Charles and Frank out of the Hamburg Fair in 1885. There are other facts that help pinpoint 1885 as the target year. First, the new grandstand was completed just before the opening of the 1884 Erie

County Fair.[17] Still, final completion did not occur until a month or more after that fair.[18] It's therefore reasonable to consider the grandstand still "new" in 1885.

What about "Andrew Klein"? The only mention of a butcher named "Andrew Klein" told of his opening a butcher shop at 230 Sherman Street in the city of Buffalo.[19] Two very good reasons exist why Frank did not go to this Andrew Klein. First, it was quite a distance to travel to the City of Buffalo from Hamburg. Second, this Andrew Klein didn't open his shop until 1891.

Does this knock out the Menches brothers? Nope. It turns out, as reported (very quickly we might add) by others,[20] Kunzog (or Frank) wrote "Klein" but meant "Stein." Andrew Stein established his meat market in the Village of Hamburg in 1866[21] and didn't sell it until 1889.[22] Furthermore, Stein was extremely well connected. He served as Chief of Police at the Erie County Fair[23] and as Supervisor of the Town of Hamburg.[24] Andrew Stein is certainly someone the young Menches boys would have been told to seek out if they needed butcher help.

But is the reason why Stein said "no" to slaughtering the pig valid? Firstly, the 1885 Fair drew record breaking crowds with the peak being September 17th.[25] Given that, it would make sense the Menches brothers would have exhausted their supply of sausage, necessitating a trip to Andrew Stein's meat market. Now, bear in mind, with no refrigeration technology, daily weather conditions were more important back then. In reviewing the meteorological records during the 1885 fair, we can pinpoint one day where it was "unusually hot and humid." According to data obtained from the National Oceanic and Atmospheric Administration, the 1885 Erie County Fair showed temperatures rising each day, peaking on September 18th. The high temperature hovered about 4 degrees above the previous 13-year average and the low temperature nearly 10 degrees hotter than average. Furthermore, local newspaper reports indicate the high temperature that day was reached around noon with the humidity pushing above 90%.[26]

While the prevailing weather conditions certainly support Stein's decision not to slaughter the pig, a more compelling reason existed, one that Frank (and Kunzog) might not have been familiar with. At the time of the 1885 Fair, an epidemic known as hog cholera killed off much of the local herds in Western New York.[27] Not only did this result in fewer entries in the swine class, but it might have led Stein to conclude he couldn't waste a pig.

It would be nice to report minutes exist from the Erie County Agricultural Society detailing the change in policy regarding wood and coal burning stoves. Unfortunately, records back then weren't kept as well as they're kept now.

The same thing could be said of a report of a woman's dress catching fire. If it occurred, it likely didn't cause too much harm otherwise the normally sensationalistic reporting of the era would have documented it. We do, however, see evidence of the power of the "Ladies Department" as 1885 saw the opening of a brand new "Domestic Hall" (today referred to as the "Octagon Building") on their behalf.[28]

We'll end with this vignette. One of the chief criticisms of the Menches Brothers Hamburg, N.Y. origin story is the town's name. "Hamburg? Isn't that a bit too convenient?" they might say. Compounding this perception is Kunzog's naming story, replete with the German tongue. It certainly sounds contrived, the fruit of some poetic license.

Or is it? Here's a clip from an actual newspaper report written while the 1885 Erie County Fair was still in progress:

"E.B. Brown and wife of Prospect Avenue took in the fair yesterday. At dinner time they repaired to the spacious dining room under the grand stand. Mr. Brown being rather hungry inquired if they had any vegetables. 'Oh, yah,' replied the proprietor. 'Ve always keeps a big shupply of do Hamburg cheese. Do vas mine choicest vegetable!'"[29]

The reporter mimics the German dialect as best he could. Meanwhile, lest you believe "Hamburg Cheese" to be of German origin, it was the name commonly applied to cheese coming from Western New York-based dairies (initially Hamburg, N.Y.). Its popularity peaked just before the Civil War.[30] If "Hamburg cheese" was named after the town of Hamburg, N.Y., why not the "Hamburg sandwich"?

The circumstantial evidence for the Menches hamburger origin story is very strong. How might all this have actually taken place? Find out in the concluding episode…

A Day In Hamburger History – September 18, 1885 – Everything is the Same, Except, "You Are There!"

CHAPTER SEVENTEEN:
A DAY IN HAMBURGER HISTORY
– SEPTEMBER 18, 1885 –

"What sort of day was it? A day like all days, filled with those events that alter and illuminate our times... all things are as they were then, and you were there."
— Walter Cronkite, at the conclusion of each episode of the CBS Series *You Are There*

On this day, September 18th, 1885, the last day of the Erie County Fair, Hiram P. Hopkins woke up to threatening skies. While the weather appeared ominous, he breathed a sigh of relief. He didn't see the clouds as presaging rain. Rather, he saw the southwesterly breeze as ushering in unusually warm temperatures. In exchange, he'd accept the oppressive humidity.

In the early morning, before the expected thousands of fairgoers arrived, Hiram strolled the grounds. Just a day earlier, the place was packed, the crowd so dense it was difficult to move. This morning the only people Hopkins could see were the many vendors prepping their booths for the final day. Popcorn, peanuts and candy sellers had a brisk business the day before. The same was true of those selling lemonade, pop, and sandwiches.

As he passed close to the grandstand, he noticed two young men fretting about. They were the Menches brothers from Canton, Ohio. Still in their twenties, Hiram took a liking to Charles and Frank. They reminded him of another young man – himself. Their innovativeness impressed him. Unlike the older vendors, they used newer and safer gas burning stoves. They also specialized in only one kind of sandwich – a pork sausage sandwich. This set them apart from the many ham sandwich stands.

Hiram went up to Charles, the older of the two. "What's troubling you, boys?" he asked.

It was so busy the day before, the brothers had sold out of their signature sandwich. "We're out of pork sausage," said Charles. "Do you know where we can get more?"

Hopkins pondered this for a moment. He remembered former Hamburg Supervisor Andrew Stein had a butcher shop not too far away in the Village of Hamburg. "Have you tried Stein's Meat Market in the Village?" offered Hiram.

Frank Menches looked up at the clouds. He may have been only twenty, but as a competitive bicycle racer, he knew how to read the clouds. And the wind. It was blowing stiffly from the southwest, pushing up warm moist air from his Ohio hometown. It was going to rain. Yesterday was a banner day. He wasn't sure about today. But he trusted his older brother. If Charles said the people will come rain or shine, then the people will come. Still, he didn't want to order too much pork sausage.

Frank arrived at the meat market on Main Street. He walked in. He was not surprised to see someone there this early in the morning. "Hello," said Frank. "I'm Frank Menches. My brother and I have a booth at the Fair selling pork sausage sandwiches. We've run out of meat. Mr. Hiram Hopkins suggested we inquire of Mr. Andrew Stein if we might purchase ten pounds of pork."

"Well, I'm Mr. Stein," said the man behind the counter. "That's not a lot of meat. It doesn't make sense for me to slaughter an entire pig. I'm not sure I'd be able to sell the rest and it's too hot and humid for me to keep it too long." Stein held back the real reason. With the hog cholera epidemic, he simply didn't have the pigs to spare.

"What am I to do?" asked Frank.

"Have you tried ground beef?" suggested Stein. "I can chop up ten pounds for you."

Frank thought about this for a moment. He and his brother had specialized in pork sausage sandwiches. Furthermore, he feared his customers would look down on ground beef. While accepted for its medicinal value (it was believed to be easier to digest), it wasn't highly regarded by the class of people who typically ventured to county fairs.

"Better make it only five pounds," replied Frank. "It looks like rain and, with the final race to close the Fair coming shortly after lunch, I'm not sure how much we'll be able to sell today."

Frank left Andrew Stein's meat market with the small package. He looked above to the clouds. The skies were no longer threatening. They were raining. The heavy downpour muddied the way back to the Fair. Frank sloshed his way to the Menches Brothers white tent.

Charles looked up and saw Frank approaching. "A smaller package? Good choice," said the older brother. "The rain will keep people away – at least for now."

Frank plopped the hunk of meat on the plank and opened it. "Then that will give us some time to determine what to do with this," said Frank as he revealed the ground beef concealed by the butcher paper.

Frank fired up the stove as Charles eyed the meat. "Well," said Charles, "if we can't have pork sausage patties, we may as well try ground beef patties." He pulled a handful of meat from the ball and formed a patty. When the griddle seemed the right temperature, he placed the patty on the hot iron. The brothers watched it fry. Its sweet smelling juices teased their nostrils. Once it got good and brown on the outside, they took the primordial hamburger off the grill and sampled it.

It had no taste. Worse, it wasn't cooked on the inside. "How are we going to cook the middle without burning the outside?" asked Frank.

Charles contemplated this dilemma. "How about if we add some coffee beans to the inside," he said. "When they bake, they'll steam the interior and cook it."

The brothers tried this. They pulled this next attempt off the grill. They tasted it. Their faces winced. "At least it's now cooked all the way through," said Frank.

"Yes, but it tastes awful," said Charles. "Let's try adding brown sugar and maybe a few other of these ingredients."

It worked. The mix of spices and flavors created a tasty sandwich suited for candy concessionaires. The skies cleared by 11 o'clock. Thousands of people decided to venture to the fair in time for the 1 o'clock parade of livestock. The marquee race – a free-for-all – would immediately ensue.

Once again, a dense crowd formed, particularly in front of the new grandstand. The Menches brothers' stand, like the day before, became a flurry of activity. They barely had time to come up with a catchy carnival barker shout to convince fairgoers to purchase their new concoction.

When it comes to the Erie County Fair, though, people will often buy something simply because it's for sale. Especially when there's a lot of people around the booth. Fortunately, the Menches brothers also sold candy, peanuts and popcorn confections. That attracted the crowd. They only had enough ground beef to make 75 hamburgers – although that includes the burgers used in their initial testing. The new sandwich proved popular.

With barely a breather during the lunchtime rush, Frank and Charles didn't have the luxury (or the need) to contemplate the significance of their innovative culinary invention. To them, it was simply a ground beef sandwich. It was merely a product they needed to sell at a certain price to make enough profit to insure their business remained sustainable. That their customized additional ingredients made it something different didn't occur to them.

Until a particularly satisfied customer came up to Frank and said in broken German-English, "Das ist gut! Vas ist?"

The question shocked Frank. He hadn't thought of a name. But he knew he needed to respect the compliment of a customer with an answer. He looked up at the nearby grandstand. There in the vicinity hung a banner with the phrase "Hamburg Fair." Frank looked at the happy customer and said, "We call it a Hamburg sandwich."

And with that, the world's second greatest invention – and a trillion-dollar business – was born.

It turns out this wouldn't be the only time the Menches brothers would have a significant impact on the history of confectionary edibles. One of the first big-time corporate concessionaires in an era when concessions became a real business, Charles and Frank Menches often found themselves in a position to be "the first" in many things.

Alas, time eventually erodes the memory of these "firsts." The years create a distance so vast these memories ultimately fade and disappear. Even descendants can fall prey to this amnesia. Until something out of the blue triggers a small spark. Relive the magic of just such a spark in our closing epilogue…

A Family Rediscovers Itself

EPILOGUE:
A FAMILY REDISCOVERS ITSELF

After years of imagining what was inside, Judy Kusmits finally unlocked and opened the forbidden door. Judy's grandmother Felicia had always kept those doors locked. She never allowed anyone to touch it.

The "it" was a mahogany buffet. The one with four stout legs and a silver tray on top. It was an old thing. Felicia bought it when she lived on Miller Avenue in the 1940s. It had a matching table and china cabinet. And drawers. Drawers filled with, well, only Felicia knew for sure.

When Felicia passed away in 1972, Judy's mother Gloria kept with Felicia's rule. It's not that Judy and her siblings didn't ever get a glimpse at what was inside those drawers. A few years before at Christmas, Gloria had passed out as gifts some of the items long stashed within this antique artifact. She gave Judy's brother John and his wife Mary the McKinley inaugural plate. Judy received a few pieces of silver.

Sadly, mom had just passed away. The time had now come for the children to see what remained hidden in this family heirloom

Small treasures mostly. Their grandfather's glasses. A watch. Chinaware. Nothing valuable to speak of.

Nestled within these trinkets they found an unimpressive piece of folded brown paper. It looked and felt not unlike the kind of paper a butcher would use to wrap meat. Curious, Judy opened it. She immediately knew exactly what was.

It was the Holy Grail.

*   *   *   *   *

One day, while attending Lakeview Elementary School in the early 1950s, Ron Bush's teacher gave the entire class a particularly challenging homework assignment. Typical of such projects for that age, the students were asked to write a story of a person of importance. Ron chose his grandfather.

"Pops," as Ron called him, was a very big man. He was also a better than average practical joker. Ron had a lot of fun with Pops, especially when the two went fishing. But that wasn't the reason why Ron wanted to write about Pops. Even at that young age, Ron knew Pops had made some major contributions not just to his family and the local community, but to America itself. Pops was Frank Menches, and Ron was his grandson.

Ron wrote appreciatively of his grandfather's role in introducing to Americans not only the hamburger, but also the ice cream cone and "Gee-Whiz" Carmel Popcorn, (the predecessor of "Crackerjacks"). Ron was only about six years old when Frank told his grandson the story of the various Menches brothers businesses. Ron was proud to be related to this man.

His classmates, however, were not so kind. Even when presented with "proof," they didn't believe Ron and teased him tirelessly about his claim.

Judy, Ron's younger cousin (by four years), found herself subject to the same treatment. Judy is Charles Menches great-granddaughter. Her grandfather, Charles' son Harry, died before Judy was born. She learned the family history from her grandmother. Around the time of Frank's death in 1951, her grandmother explained to Judy how "Pop" (both Charles and Frank were called Pop by their respective families) had travelled to the Erie County Fair in Hamburg, New York. It was there they discovered the idea of the hamburger sandwich.

A year or so later, when she was in kindergarten at Spicer School on Carroll Street in Akron, Judy was very excited to relay to her teacher the Menches role in popular foods. Miss Catherine encouraged her to tell the whole class. Judy did. She told the story exactly as her grandmother had told it to her.

"Such an outlandish thing to tell everyone!!!" Judy now recalls. "The kids all laughed and said it couldn't be true." The next day she brought in a Kenny Nichols column from the *Akron Beacon Journal* as proof. Miss

Catherine read it aloud to the class. "This took a bit of the sting out of my embarrassment," says Judy, "but I was careful not to mention our family history any further in school, at least for a while." After that, she learned to always take her proof with her if she wanted to talk about the hamburger or the ice cream cone.

Newspapers continued to reprint various (and often conflicting) stories about the Menches brothers' role in the creation of both the hamburger and the ice cream cone. The hamburger story, for the most part, remained local, but the ice cream cone story stayed in the national spotlight.

Once, when he was in the Navy, Ron saw a national story that claimed someone other than the Menches brothers invented the ice cream cone. Ron had come to rely on his father Cecil as the keeper of the Menches brothers's story. Armed with his father's notes, Ron convinced a national press syndicate to distribute the Menches brothers' ice cream cone story. This was in the 1970s.

In 1985, a retired school teacher named Iola Kimmel approached the Hamburg, New York Chamber of Commerce and began hawking a magazine article from a now out-of-print publication that featured historical trivia. This article may have been older than five years at the time, but it contained something very interesting. It told the story of how the Menches Brothers had invented the hamburger at the Erie County Fair in 1885. Through this article, folks in Hamburg discovered John C. Kunzog's book *Tanbark and Tinsel*.

With the 100-year anniversary approaching, the Chamber of Commerce got into action. Their anniversary festival soon made national news.

Gloria saw it first. She was watching the evening news when the "Hamburger turns 100" piece appeared. She immediately called Judy and told her what she just saw. "I remember that I stayed up to catch the 11 o'clock news to see if the story was repeated and it was!!!!" says Judy. "We were all excited about the coverage. The next day I reached out to the Hamburg Chamber of Commerce with our version of the story. They had tried to validate the story by looking for Charles and Frank in New

York. They were quite surprised when I explained that our family were concessionaires from Ohio."

Shortly after that, Ron's father told him about the news from Hamburg. "I was just retired from the Naval service and living in Connecticut," says Ron. "I received a phone call from my father telling all about how the Menches family was on the road to telling the nation about where and how there was a 'Hamburger.' I was happy for the Menches family and thought they deserved much recognition and praise."

Judy quickly became the family archivist, collecting as much original material as she could. That was a challenge. With very large and extended families for both Charles and Frank, much of the family history was discarded.

The various versions of the Menches brothers' hamburger origin story presented a further challenge. Judy tried her best to correct the record. "Most of the articles are not correct especially if the source was incorrect," she says. "Even when I tried to give our story many details went back to the original source and I was very clear about the errors."

Judy was able to track down Catherine Kunzog Wright in Jamestown, New York. She was the daughter of John C. Kunzog. She didn't have much except for an atticful of books. Judy asked, "Can I buy one?"

Catherine replied, "You can buy them all. I don't have anyone to give them to." So Judy left Jamestown with three boxes of Tanbark and Tinsel.

But that just got her back to square one. What she really wanted to find in all her family records was the Holy Grail, definitive proof of the Menches brothers' hamburger story she had been told since before she went to kindergarten.

In 1989, Gloria died. As the children cleaned out her belongings, attention turned to the buffet. As long as they could remember, the ancient buffet was the "forbidden fruit" of the Menches household. No one was permitted to open its locked doors except Felicia.

That fateful day, when Gloria's offspring gathered to inventory her estate, the time had come to finally free the mysterious contents from their prison within the buffet. What they found were items of little intrinsic value. Yet what they did find warmed their hearts. "We didn't think too much of anything because there wasn't much of great value," says Judy. "It's funny. When you don't have a lot of heirlooms, the smallest things can be so important."

Then they came to the brown parchment-like paper. When Judy unfolded it and read what was written upon it, she instantly knew what it was. "I knew right away it was a recipe for the burger!!!" says Judy, "There was a recipe written on brown paper, ground up beef with coffee and seasoning. I was just so happy to know that we had an original formula for our famous sandwich!!!!"

Of course, they had to try it out immediately.

With this little piece of paper – this trigger – a fountain of forgotten memories gushed forth. A family long ago separated by time and largesse, came together to honor those who had come before them.

The Menches Brothers were reborn.

$$*\qquad*\qquad*\qquad*\qquad*$$

Author's Coda:

I had been to far too many Boy Scout camping trips to trust the communal cleaning stations. The process includes three buckets – essentially "Disinfect," "Wash," and "Rinse." I quickly learned to avoid using utensils at all costs. It was sandwiches or shish-ka-bobs or nothing.

Hot dogs, hamburgers, and similar sandwich meats made lunch and dinner easy. Breakfast, however, proved the greater challenge.

Until, one morning, when a notion suddenly struck. It was so obvious, I wondered why I had never thought of it before.

Here's what it was:

I'd scramble an egg and cook it like an omelet, only folding it into a size small enough to fit comfortably between two 4-inch diameter pancakes. I had created a new form of breakfast sandwich. The boys were amazed. They had never seen anything like it before. They began making it themselves. Sure, the pancakes might have been a little hot to hold at first, but if it got them out of cleaning their utensils, it was worth the price.

I never named the sandwich. Neither did the boys. It wasn't so much an invention as it was a solution.

Little did we know that, a few years earlier, McDonald's began offering their "McGriddle Sandwich" – essentially the same thing.

That I wasn't the first to use pancakes as the bread and eggs as the meat of a new breakfast sandwich doesn't bother me. It certainly doesn't prevent me from enjoying the fruits of serendipity. It has never, and never will, make me feel less creative.

Perhaps the same could be said for all of our suspects.

FOOTNOTES

Chapter 1: The Question That Changed History

[1] Indeed, the skies were threatening that morning, according to local newspaper reports. Still, consider this chapter a dramatic recreation of the known historical record, with a dash of poetic license thrown in for theatrical effect. The weather, the life of Hiram P. Hopkins, and the events involving the 1885 Erie County Fair all come from contemporary sources. Alas, the actual question referenced in the title evolves from speculative conclusions based on secondary sources. Still, it very well might have happened exactly as the story unfolds in this opening prelude to what amounts to a rigorous academic exercise. – Author

Chapter 2: Mankind's (Second) Greatest Invention

[1] "We Aim to Please," Popeye the Sailorpedia, accessed February, 8, 2018, http://popeye.wikia.com/wiki/We_Aim_to_Please.

[2] White Castle "Our Story," White Castle, accessed August 5, 2018, https://www.whitecastle.com/about/company/our-story.

[3] "We Aim to Please," Popeye the Sailorpedia, accessed February, 8, 2018, http://popeye.wikia.com/wiki/We_Aim_to_Please.

[4] Kiri Tannenbaum, "Fast-Food Firsts: A History of American Restaurants, Doughnut Shops, and Convenience Stores," *Delish*, June 2015.

[5] Donna Scanlon, "McDonald's Bar-B-Que?" *Library of Congress*, May 2010.

[6] Scanlon, "McDonald's Bar-B-Que?" *Library of Congress*, May 2010.

[7] John R. Schermerhorn Jr., *Exploring Management* (Hoboken, N.J.: John Wiley & Sons, Inc., 2007)

[8] "History," In-N-Out Burger, accessed August 5, 2018, http://www.in-n-out.com/history.aspx.

[9] Beth Dippel, "Sheboygan County history arrived here in 1958," *Sheboygan Press* (Sheboygan, Wisconsin), June 13, 2014.

[10] Harrison Smith "David Edgerton, Burger King co-founder who helped make the Whopper, dies at 90," *Washington Post* (Washington, District of Columbia), April 18, 2018.

[11] "History of Burger King," Fast Food Menu Prices, accessed June 20, 2018, https://www.fastfoodmenuprices.com/history-of-burger-king/.

[12] "McDonald's Corporation," Reference for Business, accessed August 5, 2018, https://www.referenceforbusiness.com/businesses/M-Z/McDonald-s-Corporation.html.

[13] Don Daszkowski, "Learn the History of Wendy's – How David Thomas Built Kentucky Fried Chicken and Wendy's," *The Balance Small Business*, August 12, 2017, https://www.thebalancesmb.com/dave-thomas-of-kentucky-fried-chicken-wendys-1350962.

[14] "History of Wendy's Restaurant," *Food History*, January 8, 2014, https://www.world-foodhistory.com/2014/01/history-of-wendys-restaurant.html.

[15] Tannenbaum, "Fast-Food Firsts: A History of American Restaurants, Doughnut Shops, and Convenience Stores," *Delish*, June 2015.

[16] Rupert Neate, "McDonald's: a brief history in 15 facts," *The Guardian* (Kings Place, London), May 2, 2015.

[17] Archeologists in Pompeii, Italy, may have uncovered what they believe might have been a roadside food service business, perhaps the first recorded example of a fast food restaurant. – *Author's personal on-site observation*

[18] "Fast Food Industry Analysis 2018 - Cost & Trends," Franchise Help, accessed August 5, 2018, https://www.franchisehelp.com/industry-reports/fast-food-industry-analysis-2018-cost-trends/.

[19] "Fast Food Industry Analysis 2018 - Cost & Trends," Franchise Help, accessed August 5, 2018, https://www.franchisehelp.com/industry-reports/fast-food-industry-analysis-2018-cost-trends/.

[20] "Number of employees in the United States fast food restaurant industry from 2004 to 2018*," Statista, accessed August, 5, 2018, https://www.statista.com/statistics/196630/number-of-employees-in-us-fast-food-restaurants-since-2002/.

[21] What is the most important invention in mankind's history? Why, the wheel, of course. And because the automobile played such a critical role in the growth of the fast food business, you can see how the most important invention (the wheel) and the second most important invention (the hamburger) combined to create arguably the world's most important business (in terms of the number of people it directly impacts). - *Author*

Chapter 3: Those Amazing Menches Boys

[1] "Picnics," *Stark County Democrat* (Canton, Ohio), July 14, 1881.

[2] H.B. (Doc) Kerr, "Around the Town," *Akron Beacon Journal* (Akron, Ohio), December 6, 1938.

[3] "A Field Day – Bicycle Races," *The Stark County Democrat* (Canton, Ohio), July 9, 1885.

[4] "The Salem Tournament," *The Stark County Democrat* (Canton, Ohio), July 8, 1886.

[5] John Menches and Ron Bush in discussion with the author, October 19, 2017.

[6] Kerr, "Around the Town," *Akron Beacon Journa* (Akron, Ohio)*l*, December 6, 1938.

[7] "Burglars Make a Haul," *Stark County Democrat* (Canton, Ohio), April 17, 1884.

[8] Advertisement, *Stark County Democrat (a.k.a. "Canton News-Democrat")* (Canton, Ohio), Wednesday, July 3, 1895.

[9] John Menches and Ron Bush in discussion with the author, October 19, 2017.

[10] "Menches & Barber's Circus. – Undoubtedly the Best Equipped Cheap Circus on the Road," *Stark County Democrat* (Canton, Ohio), April 21, 1887.

[11] "A Circus Split – Barber Wants a Receiver for the Menches & Barber Show," *Stark County Democrat (a.k.a. "Canton News-Democrat")* (Canton, Ohio), October 20, 1887.

[12] "Around the Town with H.B. (Doc) Kerr," *Akron Beacon Journal* (Akron, Ohio), December 31, 1938.

[13] "County Fair," *Stark County Democrat* (Canton, Ohio), September 12, 1889.

[14] Kerr, "Around the Town," *Akron Beacon Journal* (Akron, Ohio), December 6, 1938.

[15] John Kunzog, *Tanbark and Tinsel: A Galaxy of Glittering Gems from the Dazzling Diadem of Circus History* (Jamestown, NY: John C. Kinzog, 1970).

[16] John Menches and Ron Bush in discussion with the author, October 19, 2017.

[17] Carroll D. Wright, *Industrial Depressions: The First Annual Report of the United States Commissioner of Labor* (Washington, DC: Government Printing Office; 1886), 65-66.

[18] "Around the Town with H.B. (Doc) Kerr," *Akron Beacon Journal* (Akron, Ohio), December 5, 1938.

[19] Advertisement, *Akron Daily Democrat* (Akron, Ohio), May 19, 1899.

[20] "Ball Park – At Summit Lake Changing Hands. – Menches Bros. Buy It of the N.O.T. Co.," *Akron Daily Democrat* (Akron, Ohio), May 13, 1901.

[21] "Great Crowd at Fair," *Akron Daily Democrat* (Akron, Ohio), October 2, 1902.

[22] John Menches and Ron Bush in discussion with the author, October 19, 2017.

[23] "Menches Brothers – Former Canton Merchants are Bankrupt," *The Stark County Democrat* (Canton, Ohio), January 19, 1904.

[24] "Want to be Discharged," *The Akron Beacon Journal* (Akron, Ohio), February 25, 1904.

[25] "Navy Chief Traces Ice Cream Cone's Origin to Grandfather," *Olean Time Herald* (Olean, New York), May 18, 1979.

[26] John Menches and Ron Bush in discussion with the author, October 19, 2017.

[27] "Baking-iron for ice-cream cones," U.S. Patent Office, App/Pub Number US9243384A, accessed September 25, 2018, https://patents.google.com/patent/US924484A/en.

[28] "Navy Chief Traces Ice Cream Cone's Origin to Grandfather," *Olean Time Herald* (Olean, New York), May 18, 1979.

[29] John Menches and Ron Bush in discussion with the author, October 19, 2017.

[30] "Opening of the New Liberty Theater," *The Akron Beacon Journal* (Akron, Ohio), December 13, 1917.

[31] "America's Own!" *The Decatur Herald* (Decatur, Illinois), December 8, 1931.

[32] "Frank Menches Dies, Invented Hamburger," *The Akron Beacon Journal* (Akron, Ohio), October 4, 1951.

[33] "Genesis of Cone" (Elkhart Truth), *The Times* (Munster, Indiana), January 25, 1932.

Chapter 4: Charles Nagreen, a.k.a., "Hamburger Charlie"

[1] "Interview with Emil Wurm," Home of the Hamburger, accessed October 27, 2018, http://www.homeofthehamburger.org/interview-with-emil.

[2] Robert C. Nesbit. *Wisconsin: A History* (Wisconsin: University of Wisconsin Press, 1989), 15.

[3] "Called Home – A Pioneer Woman of Medina," *The Neenah Daily Times* (Neenah, Wisconsin), January 18, 1908.

[4] "A Famous Old House," *The Appleton Crescent* (Appleton, Wisconsin), March 22, 1902.

[5] "Medina Village Got Its Name From Early Emigrants From Ohio," *The Post-Crescent* (Appleton, Wisconsin), June 15, 1923.

[6] "The Usual New Year's Dance," *The Appleton Crescent* (Appleton, Wisconsin), November 30, 1878.

[7] "Personal," *The Appleton Crescent* (Appleton, Wisconsin), July 12, 1890.

[8] "Brevities," *The Post-Crescent* (Appleton, Wisconsin), February 18, 1901.

[9] "The City," *The Neenah Daily Times* (Neenah, Wisconsin), March 13, 1896.

[10] "Brevities," *The Appleton Crescent* (Appleton, Wisconsin), March 21, 1896.

[11] "Some Truth, But Not So Much – Medina Romance Which Comes by Way of Missouri," *The Post-Crescent* (Appleton, Wisconsin), July 31, 1901.

[12] "A Fake – The Andrew Rhoades Yarn," *The Neenah Daily Times* (Neenah, Wisconsin), August 1, 1901.

[13] "Medina," *The Appleton Crescent* (Appleton, Wisconsin), July 15, 1904.

[14] "Medina," *Appleton Post* (Appleton, Wisconsin), September 1, 1905.

[15] "Medina," *The Appleton Crescent* (Appleton, Wisconsin), June 4, 1904.

[16] "Short Notes," *The Oshkosh Northwestern* (Oshkosh, Wisconsin), March 11, 1905.

[17] "Called Home – A Pioneer Woman of Medina," *The Neenah Daily Times* (Neenah, Wisconsin), January 18, 1908.

[18] Thomas Henry Ryan, *History of Outagamie County Wisconsin* (Chicago: Goodspeed Historical Association Publishers, 1911), 838, 950-951.

[19] M. A. W. Brown and Hiram O. Brown, *Soldiers' and Citizens' Album of Biographical Record, Containing Personal Sketches of Army Men and Citizens Prominent in Loyalty of the Union* (Chicago: Grand Army Publishing Company, 1888), 185-186.

[20] Brown and Brown, *Soldiers' and Citizens' Album of Biographical Record, Containing Personal Sketches of Army Men and Citizens Prominent in Loyalty of the Union* (Chicago: Grand Army Publishing Company, 1888), 186.

[21] Ryan, *History of Outagamie County Wisconsin* (Chicago: Goodspeed Historical Association Publishers, 1911), 950-951.

[22] Bill Knutson, "It was a hamburger, he said," *The Post-Crescent* (Appleton, Wisconsin), Nov 9, 1985.

[23] "Our Country Neighbors – Shiocton," *Appleton Post* (Appleton, Wisconsin), March 13, 1890.

[24] "Appleton Pleasure Club Excursion," *The Menasha Record* (Menasha, Wisconsin), August 9, 1917.

[25] Advertisement, *The Post-Crescent* (Appleton, Wisconsin), June 14, 1919.

[26] Advertisement, *The Post-Crescent* (Appleton, Wisconsin), June 27, 1919.

[27] "City News," *The Post-Crescent* (Appleton, Wisconsin), August 30, 1919.

[28] "Well, done, Seymour – City stakes claim as home of hamburger," *Wisconsin State Journal* (Madison, Wisconsin), December 21, 1988.

[29] Knutson, "It was a hamburger, he said," *The Post-Crescent* (Appleton, Wisconsin), Nov 9, 1985.

[30] "Interview with Emil Wurm," Home of the Hamburger, accessed October 27, 2018, http://www.homeofthehamburger.org/interview-with-emil.

Chapter 5: Louis Lassen and Louis' Lunch

[1] "History of the Army Wagon," Hansen Wheel & Wagon Shop, accessed October 27, 2018, https://www.hansenwheel.com/history-of-the-army-wagon.

[2] "Hamburger Trivia," Iowa Beef Industry Council, accessed October 27, 2018, https://www.iabeef.org/Media/IABeef/Docs/hamburgertrivia.pdf.

[3] *The Goodnight-Loving Trail,* Produced by the Humble Oil & Refining Company in cooperation with the Texas Department of Public Safety (1960; Texas), video.

[4] "Chuckwagon the focus of new museum display," *The Montana Standard* (Butte, Montana), May 27, 2001.

[5] Marjorie White, "Chuckwagon Still Range Lifeline," *El Paso Times* (El Paso, Texas), October 15, 1967.

[6] Ross Phares, "Swift Progress Made by Texans," *The Marshall News Messenger* (Marshall, Texas), November 17, 1954.

[7] "Oklahoman Has Story On Longhorn Days," *The Daily Oklahoman* (Oklahoma City, Oklahoma), January 14, 1940. Incidentally, in 1955 the National Cowboy & Western Heritage Museum selected Charles Goodnight as one of the original five honorees voted into its Hall of Great Westerners (the other four being Jake McClure, Will Rogers, Teddy Roosevelt, and Charles Marion Russell).

[8] "Railway Improvements – A Dining Room Car to be Placed on the Michigan Central Railroad – A Description of This New Invention," *Detroit Free Press* (Detroit, Michigan), March 31, 1868.

[9] "Letter From Kansas – How a Pennsylvania Farms in Kansas," *Valley Spirit* (Chambersburg, Pennsylvania), July 24, 1878.

[10] "Ashby," *Fitchburg Sentinel* (Fitchburg, Massachusetts), October 4, 1884.

[11] "Never Goes to Sleep," *The Philadelphia Times* (Philadelphia, Pennsylvania), November 26, 1893.

[12] "Luncheons on Wheels – Curious Facts About the Restaurant Wagons Open in the Night," *The Kansas City Gazette* (Kansas City, Kansas), November 24, 1894.

[13] Colin M. Caplan, *Legendary Locals of New Haven,* (Connecticut: Arcadia Publishing, 2013), 108.

[14] "Louis Lassen", Find A Grave, accessed October 26, 2018, https://www.findagrave.com/memorial/130565397/louis-lassen.

[15] "A Great Private Park," *The Morning Courier-Journal* (New Haven, Connecticut), May 28, 1885.

[16] "Christmas Festival of the German Baptist Mission Sunday School at Bethany Chapel," *The Morning Courier-Journal* (New Haven, Connecticut), December 31, 1886.

[17] "Christian Endeavorers – of Thirty-four New Haven Societies Met Last Night – Fifteenth Anniversary of New Haven Union at Howard Ave. Congregational Church – Addresses by Pioneers of the Movement – It Originated in New Haven" *The Morning Courier-Journal* (New Haven, Connecticut), January 18, 1901.

[18] "German Republican Rally," *The Morning Courier-Journal* (New Haven, Connecticut), October 18, 1892.

[19] "To-Night's Grand Rally – Big Republican Meeting at the Hyperion," *The Morning Courier-Journal* (New Haven, Connecticut), September 23, 1893.

[20] "The Oleomargarine Law," *The Morning Courier-Journal* (New Haven, Connecticut), November 13, 1886.

[21] Mack J. Hughes, "Oleomargarine and the Constitution," *Montana Law Review*, 10, Iss. 1 (1949), 51.

[22] Caplan, *Legendary Locals of New Haven*, (Connecticut: Arcadia Publishing, 2013), 108.

[23] Advertisement, *The Yale Daily News* (New Haven, Connecticut), January 7, 1950.

[24] "Storybook Bricks Tell of Changes As Progress Moves Louis' Lunch," *The Yale Daily News* (New Haven, Connecticut), September 30, 1966.

[25] "New Haven Restaurant Claims To Have Served First Hamburger," *Bennington Banner* (Bennington, Vermont), November 24, 1967.

[26] Owen Rogers, "Louis' Lunch and the Birth of the Hamburger," Encyclopedia of Connecticut History Online, accessed October, 27, 2018, https://connecticuthistory.org/louis-lunch-and-the-birth-of-the-hamburger/.

[27] "Storybook Bricks Tell of Changes As Progress Moves Louis' Lunch," *The Yale Daily News* (new Haven, Connecticut), September 30, 1966.

[28] Tom Condon, "Owner of Louis' Lunch Hopes People Can Help Him Save It," *Hartford Courant* (Hartford, Connecticut), March 8, 1974.

[29] Rogers, "Louis' Lunch and the Birth of the Hamburger," Encyclopedia of Connecticut History Online, accessed October, 27, 2018, https://connecticuthistory.org/louis-lunch-and-the-birth-of-the-hamburger/.

[30] Tom Condon, "Hamburger's Home Reopens with Relish," *Hartford Courant* (Hartford, Connecticut), March 23, 1976.

[31] Theodore Blatchford, "Birthplace of US Hamburg Endures on Temple Street," *The Yale Daily News* (New Haven, Connecticut), November 7, 1963.

[32] "Louis Lunch waits on City Death Row," *The Yale Daily News* (New Haven, Connecticut), July 1, 1974.

[33] Blatchford, "Birthplace of US Hamburg Endures on Temple Street," *The Yale Daily News* (New Haven, Connecticut), November 7, 1963.

[34] "Louis Lunch waits on City Death Row," *The Yale Daily News* (New Haven, Connecticut), July 1, 1974.

[35] Blatchford, "Birthplace of US Hamburg Endures on Temple Street," *The Yale Daily News* (New Haven, Connecticut), November 7, 1963.

[36] Peter B. Pach, "Louis' flavor goes beyond the burger," *Hartford Courant* (Hartford, Connecticut), March 20, 1991.

Chapter 6: 1904 St. Louis World's Fair

[1] "Around the Town with H.B. (Doc) Kerr," *Akron Beacon Journal* (Akron, Ohio), December 31, 1938.

[2] "Ball Park – At Summit Lake Changing Hands. – Menches Bros. Buy It of the N.O.T. Co.," *Akron Daily Democrat* (Akron, Ohio), May 13, 1901.

[3] At least 60 advertisements in *The Akron Daily Democrat* (Akron, Ohio) from May 16, 1901 through September 7, 1901.

[4] "Around the Town with H.B. (Doc) Kerr," *Akron Beacon Journal* (Akron, Ohio), December 31, 1938.

[5] Pamela J. Vaccaro, *Beyond the Ice Cream Cone - The Whole Scoop on Food at the 1904 World's Fair*, (St. Louis: Enid Press, 2004), 12.

[6] Vaccaro, *Beyond the Ice Cream Cone - The Whole Scoop on Food at the 1904 World's Fair*, (St. Louis: Enid Press, 2004), 108-125.

[7] Vaccaro, *Beyond the Ice Cream Cone - The Whole Scoop on Food at the 1904 World's Fair*, (St. Louis: Enid Press, 2004), 110.

[8] Vaccaro, *Beyond the Ice Cream Cone - The Whole Scoop on Food at the 1904 World's Fair*, (St. Louis: Enid Press, 2004), 112.

[9] Vaccaro, *Beyond the Ice Cream Cone - The Whole Scoop on Food at the 1904 World's Fair*, (St. Louis: Enid Press, 2004), 120, 123.

[10] Vaccaro, *Beyond the Ice Cream Cone - The Whole Scoop on Food at the 1904 World's Fair*, (St. Louis: Enid Press, 2004), 119-120.

[11] "News and Gossip," *The Tennessean* (Nashville, Tennessee), November 22, 1903.

[12] "Trademarks – Registered June 21, 1904," *Official Gazette of the United States Patent Office* (Washington, District of Columbia), June 21, 1904.

[13] "Burger 'Birthplace' Faces Bulldozer," *The New York Times* (New York, New York), January 12, 1974.

Chapter 7: Fletcher Davis

[1] "Joseph Against John – Fifer at Rochelle," *The Inter Ocean* (Chicago, Illinois), September 15, 1888.

2 "Predictions on The Weather," *Chicago* Tribune (Chicago, Illinois), September 15, 1888.

3 "Fletcher Short Davis," Find A Grave, accessed October 29, 2018, https://www.findagrave.com/memorial/32930408/fletcher-short-davis.

4 Diana K. Kleiner, "Athens Title and Pottery Company," Texas State Historical Association, accessed November 3, 2018, https://tshaonline.org/handbook/online/articles/dlaun.

5 "Joseph Elmer Miller," Find A Grave, accessed November 3, 2018, https://www.findagrave.com/memorial/64936510/joseph-elmer-miller.

6 "Pearl Eli Miller," Find A Grave, accessed November 3, 2018, https://www.findagrave.com/memorial/64936005/pearl-eli-miller.

7 "Fletcher Short Davis," Find A Grave, accessed October 29, 2018, https://www.findagrave.com/memorial/32930408/fletcher-short-davis.

8 "Fletcher Short Davis," Find A Grave, accessed October 29, 2018, https://www.findagrave.com/memorial/32930408/fletcher-short-davis.

9 "Pearl Eli Miller," Find A Grave, accessed November 3, 2018, https://www.findagrave.com/memorial/64936005/pearl-eli-miller.

10 Frank X. Tolbert, *Tolbert's Texas* (Doubleday, 1983).

11 "Fletcher Short Davis," Find A Grave, accessed October 29, 2018, https://www.findagrave.com/memorial/32930408/fletcher-short-davis.

12 "Fletcher Short Davis," Find A Grave, accessed October 29, 2018, https://www.findagrave.com/memorial/32930408/fletcher-short-davis.

13 "Fletcher Short Davis," Find A Grave, accessed October 29, 2018, https://www.findagrave.com/memorial/32930408/fletcher-short-davis.

Chapter 8: Don't Rain on Our Hometown Festival

1 "What is MEANS," Black's Law Dictionary Free Online Legal Dictionary 2nd Ed., accessed November 3, 2018, https://thelawdictionary.org/means/.

2 "What is OPPORTUNITY," Black's Law Dictionary Free Online Legal Dictionary 2nd Ed., accessed November 3, 2018, https://thelawdictionary.org/opportunity/.

3 "What is MOTIVE," Black's Law Dictionary Free Online Legal Dictionary 2nd Ed., accessed November 3, 2018, https://thelawdictionary.org/motive/.

4 "What is INTENT," Black's Law Dictionary Free Online Legal Dictionary 2nd Ed., accessed November 3, 2018, https://thelawdictionary.org/intent/.

5 "Pioneer 'Hot Dog' Man and Originator of the Justly-Famous Ice Cream Cone, Tells of Catering to the Wants of Common People," *The Akron Beacon Journal* (Akron, Ohio), September 15, 1922.

6 "Hamburger Charley to Celebrate Anniversary," *The Post-Crescent* (Appleton, Wisconsin), September 26, 1934.

7 Advertisement, *The Yale Daily News* (New Haven, Connecticut), January 7, 1950.

8 Blatchford, "Birthplace of US Hamburg Endures on Temple Street," *The Yale Daily News* (New Haven, Connecticut), November 7, 1963.

[9] "Storybook Bricks Tell of Changes As Progress Moves Louis' Lunch," *The Yale Daily News* (New Haven, Connecticut), September 30, 1966.

[10] "New Haven Restaurant Claims To Have Served First Hamburger," *Bennington Banner* (Bennington, Vermont), November 24, 1967.

[11] "Development Threatens Future of Landmark," *Hartford Courant* (Hartford, Connecticut), October 27, 1973.

[12] "Burger 'Birthplace' Faces Bulldozer," *The New York Times* (New York, New York), January 12, 1974.

[13] Condon, "Owner of Louis' Lunch Hopes People Can Help Him Save It," *Hartford Courant* (Hartford, Connecticut), March 8, 1974.

[14] Walt Wheeler, "Executive Order May Save Louis' Lunch," *Naugatuck Daily News* (Naugatuck, Connecticut), May 22, 1974.

[15] Jonathan Kaufman, "Burgers' are Back: Louis Lunch Lives!" *The Yale Daily News* (New Haven, Connecticut), September 4, 1975.

[16] Frank X. Tolbert, "Tolbert's Texas – Hamburger 'Invented' In Athens Drug Store?," *Dallas Morning News* (Dallas, Texas), February 3, 1974.

[17] Frank X. Tolbert, "A Texan, Fletcher Davis, 'invented' the hamburger," *Dallas Morning News* (Dallas, Texas), July 18, 1976.

Chapter 10 – Identify the Weapon

[1] E.V. Durling, "On the Side – Now Young Men Are Warned," *The San Francisco Examiner* (San Francisco, California), October 10, 1953.

[2] "Obituary – Dr. James H. Salisbury," *New York Tribune* (New York, New York), August 24, 1905.

[3] "Death List of a Day – Dr. James H. Salisbury," *The New York Times* (New York, New York), August 24, 1905.

[4] Logan Clendening, "Health Column – Fasting Fad Harms Few," *The Mercury* (Pottstown, Pennsylvania), May 24, 1943.

[5] W.M. Hepburn, "Correspondence – Salisbury Steak and Treatment," *Medical and Surgical Journal (Philadelphia, Pennsylvania),* January 10, 1885.

[6] "Sunbeams," *The Sun* (New York, New York), January 17, 1885.

[7] "Table Talk," *The Buffalo Commercial* (Buffalo, New York), January 22, 1885.

[8] "A Surgical Success," *The Canton Independent-Sentinel* (Canton, Pennsylvania), May 21, 1886.

[9] "A Nest of Cranks – How Dr. Salisbury of Hot Water Fame, Starves His Patients – Hollow-Eyed Human Dupes Who Imagine They are Being Cured – He Promises to Make Woman Beautiful, With Eyes Like Stars and Skins Like Babies, So All the World Will Fall at Their Feet – The Salisbury Steak," *St. Louis Post-Dispatch* (St. Louis, Missouri), May 27, 1894.

[10] "The 'Salisbury Diet'," *The Los Angeles Times Illustrated Weekly* (Los Angeles, California), September 20, 1908.

[11] "A Nest of Cranks – How Dr. Salisbury of Hot Water Fame, Starves His Patients – Hollow-Eyed Human Dupes Who Imagine They are Being Cured – He Promises to Make Woman Beautiful, With Eyes Like Stars and Skins Like Babies, So All the World Will Fall at Their Feet – The Salisbury Steak," *St. Louis Post-Dispatch* (St. Louis, Missouri), May 27, 1894.

[12] "TOWARD SUNSET. – VIII. –Summering on the Western Coast," *The Evening Star* (Washington, District of Columbia), July 22, 1872.

[13] "Anderson's European Hotel – Restaurant Bill of Fare," *The Chicago Daily Tribune* (Chicago, Illinois), July 6, 1873.

[14] "The City," *The Nebraska State Journal* (Lincoln, Nebraska), January 14, 1880.

[15] "Hamburg Steak," *Mower County Transcript* (Lansing, Minnesota), February 28, 1883.

[16] "Home and Happiness on Ten Dollars a Week," *The Eaton Democrat* (Eaton, Ohio), December 23, 1875.

[17] "Germany and the United States are constantly exchanging fish," *The Tennessean* (Nashville, Tennessee), May 3, 1883.

[18] "Same Thing," *The Progressive Age*, (Scottsboro, Alabama), December 28, 1894.

[19] "Choice and Seasonable – Valuable Receipts by a Famous and Trustworthy Authority," *The Buffalo Express* (buffalo, New York), August 4, 1885.

[20] "The Home – Choice Dishes," *The Daily Times* (Wilson, North Carolina), April 10, 1896.

[21] "Cookery Course – Schedule of Classes and Lessons Given at Mechanics Institute," *Democrat and Chronicle* (Rochester, New York), March 10, 1899.

[22] "Salisbury and Hamburger Steak," *The Boston Globe* (Boston, Massachusetts), July 30, 1911.

[23] "From Mrs. Marshall – Friday," *The Kansan* (Jamestown, Kansas), May 4, 1916.

[24] "The Observant Citizen," *The Boston Post* (Boston, Massachusetts), October 27, 1916.

[25] "Won't Serve Hamburg – No German Dishes Allowed on Dining Cars in Canada," *The Topeka State Journal* (Topeka, Kansas), September 26, 1916.

[26] Jeannette Young Norton. "Appetizing Ways to Prepare Hamburg Steak," *Messenger-Inquirer* (Owensboro, Kentucky), December 12, 1923.

[27] Sister Mary, "Sister Mary's Kitchen," *Messenger-Inquirer* (Owensboro, Kentucky), March 27, 1923.

[28] "Manila Bill of Fare," *Bismark Weekly Tribune* (Bismark, North-Dakota), December 23, 1898.

[29] Robert Sietsema, "Two Centuries of Hamburger History in New York City – On the mysterious origins and the many evolutions of the burger," April 13, 2015, https://ny.eater.com/2015/4/13/8400697/hamburger-history-new-york.

Chapter 11 – Hamburgers – The Written Record

[1] Arnold Hamilton, "Burger bragging rights Author claims Tulsa, not Texas, as origin," *Dallas Morning News* (Dallas, Texas), April 14, 1995.

[2] "The Weber's Story...," Weber's Superior Root Beer Restaurant, accessed November 12, 2018, http://www.webersoftulsa.com/webers_story.asp.

[3] "The New Lunch Room," *The Poultney Journal* (Poultney, Vermont), April 22, 1904.

[4] "Last Day of Carnival – Ballyhoos and Barkers to Rest Their Lungs – One More Day of Merrymaking and the Elk's Jubilee Will be a Matter of History," *Davenport Republican* (davenport, Iowa), June 28, 1902.

[5] "Hamburg Men Numerous," *Princeton-Clarion Leader* (Princeton, Indiana), September 21, 1900.

[6] "Kick on Hamburg – Restaurant Men File Petition Against Street Lunch Men," *Princeton-Clarion Leader* (Princeton, Indiana), September 27, 1900.

[7] "New Haven Restaurant Claims To Have Served First Hamburger," *Bennington Banner* (Bennington, Vermont), November 24, 1967.

[8] Advertisement – "Harper and Jones," *Iowa State Bystander* (Des Moines, Iowa), September 15, 1899. (the ad ran weekly until October 27, 1899)

[9] "Crutch Breaks a Head," *The Omaha Daily Bee* (Omaha, Nebraska), November 7, 1899.

[10] "Battle With Tramps," *Princeton-Clarion Leader* (Princeton, Indiana), April 26, 1899.

[11] "Tissue of Falsehood," *Daily Public Ledger* (Maysville, Kentucky), March 20, 1898.

[12] "He Will Never Know Why – Finn, Who Couldn't Be Understood, Fined by Judge Peabody," *St. Louis Dispatch* (St. Louis, Missouri), November 10, 1897.

[13] "Bisbee News – Daily Happenings at the Great Copper Camp – Budget of Interesting Items from our Regular Correspondent," *Tombstone Prospector* (Tombstone, Arizona), September 5, 1896.

[14] Bisbee News – Daily Happenings at the Great Copper Camp – Budget of Interesting Items from our Regular Correspondent," *Tombstone Prospector* (Tombstone, Arizona), September 15, 1896.

[15] "In a 'Sandwich Car.' – Phases of Human Nature as Seen by the All-Night Lunch Man," *The Chicago Tribune* (Chicago, Illinois), July 5, 1896.

[16] "Odors of the Onion – A New Night Feature of City Life – Breezes Pregnant With the Hamburger – How Curbstone Chefs Dispense Fragrant Food From Their Little Carts," *San Francisco Chronicle* (San Francisco, California), July 23, 1894.

[17] Tom Condon, "Owner of Louis' Lunch Hopes People Can Help Him Save It," *Hartford Courant* (Hartford, Connecticut), March 8, 1974.

[18] "Hamburger Sandwiches," *Reno Gazette-Journal* (Reno, Nevada), July 25, 1893.

[19] "Brevities," *Reno Gazette-Journal* (Reno, Nevada), August 25, 1893.

[20] "Not Eaten on The Premises – Hamburg Steaks and Pork Chops which cost but Little and are in Great Demand," *The Sun* (New York, New York), April 27, 1883.

[21] "The President's Progress – The Week's Record," *The Vermont Phoenix and Vermont Record and Farmer* (Brattleboro, Vermont), August 22, 1881.

22 Sarah J. Cutter, *Palatable Dishes, A Practical Guide to Good Living*, (Buffalo, N.Y.: Peter Paul & Bro., 1891), 784.

Chapter 12: The Texas Two-Step

1 D. L. Wilson, *Jefferson's Literary Commonplace Book*, (Princeton: Princeton University Press, 1989), 172.

2 Frank X. Tolbert, "Tolbert's Texas – Hamburger 'Invented' In Athens Drug Store?" *Dallas Morning News* (Dallas, Texas), February 3, 1974.

3 "Burger 'Birthplace' Faces Bulldozer," *The New York Times* (New York, New York), January 12, 1974.

4 Tolbert, "Tolbert's Texas – Hamburger 'Invented' In Athens Drug Store?" *Dallas Morning News* (Dallas, Texas), February 3, 1974.

5 Josh Ozersky, "Want lies with that?" *Los Angeles Times* (Los Angeles, California), January 29, 2007.

6 Vaccaro, *Beyond the Ice Cream Cone - The Whole Scoop on Food at the 1904 World's Fair*, (St. Louis: Enid Press, 2004), 117.

7 Gary Cartwright, "The World's First Hamburger," *Texas Monthly* (Austin, Texas), August 2009.

8 Cartwright, "The World's First Hamburger," *Texas Monthly* (Austin. Texas), August 2009.

9 "Fletcher Short Davis," Find A Grave, accessed October 29, 2018, https://www.findagrave.com/memorial/32930408/fletcher-short-davis.

10 Kent Biffle, "Time to chew on some chili and burger yore," *Dallas Morning News* (Dallas, Texas), October 30, 1994.

11 Tolbert, "Tolbert's Texas – Hamburger 'Invented' In Athens Drug Store?" *Dallas Morning News* (Dallas, Texas), April 1, 1976.

12 "Locals," *Shiner Gazette*, (Shiner, Texas), April 12, 1894. [ran weekly through September 6, 1894]

13 Arnold Hamilton, "Burger bragging rights Author claims Tulsa, not Texas, as origin," *Dallas Morning News* (Dallas, Texas), April 14, 1995.

Chapter 13 – Deconstructing the St. Louis Hamburger Origin Story

1 "Burger's Birthday," *Rocky Mount Telegram* (Rocky Mount, North Carolina), September 15, 2004.

2 "Who really 'invented' hamburger? Hamburger Cook-off," *Journal Gazette* (Mattoon, Illinois), June 5, 1979; *The Gazette* (Montreal, Quebec, Canada), June 6, 1979; *Citizens' Voice* (Wilkes-Barre, Pennsylvania), June 6, 1979; *The Herald* (Crystal Lake, Illinois), June 6, 1979; *Muncie Press* (Muncie, Indiana), June 12, 1979; *The Springfield News-Leader* (Springfield, Missouri), June 13, 1979; *The Sentinel* (Carlisle, Pennsylvania), June 13, 1979; *The Times-News* (Twin Falls, Idaho), June 13, 1979; *The Press Democrat* (Santa Rosa, California), June 13, 1979; *The Indianapolis Star* (Indianapolis, Indiana), June 13, 1979; *Fort*

Lauderdale News (Fort Lauderdale, Florida), June 13, 1979; *The Palm Beach Post* (Palm Beach, Florida), June 14, 1979; *The Atlanta Constitution* (Atlanta, Georgia), June 14, 1979; *The Tribune* (Seymour, Indiana), June 14, 1979; *The Tampa Tribune* (Tampa, Florida), June 14, 1979; *Latrobe Bulletin* (Latrobe, Pennsylvania), June 18, 1979; *Tampa Bay Times* (tampa Bay, Florida), June 21, 1979; *The Galveston News* (Galveston, Texas), June 21, 1979; *The Town Talk* (Alexandria, Louisiana), June 24, 1979; *The Pantagraph* (Bloomington, Illinois), June 27, 1979; *The Dispatch* (Moline, Illinois), July 1, 1979; *The Honolulu Advertiser* (Honolulu, Hawaii), July 22, 1979; *Honolulu Star-Bulletin* (Honolulu, Hawaii), July 22, 1979; *The Greenville News* (Greenville, South Carolina), July 22, 1979; *The Minneapolis Star* (Minneapolis, Minnesota), July 23, 1980.

[3] Ozersky, "Want lies with that?" *Los Angeles Times* (Los Angeles, California), January 29, 2007.

[4] Paul Weingarten, "The hamburger's rise to fame and fortune," *The Des Moines Register* (Des Moines, Iowa), April 6, 1977.

[5] Craig Claiborne, "Hamburger claims many inventors," *Dallas Morning News* (Dallas, Texas), May 27, 1976.

[6] Jack Maguire, "Talk of Texas – Texan invented the Hamburger," *Irving Daily News* (Irving, Texas), December 1, 1974; *Del Rio (Texas) News-Herald* (Del Rio, Texas), December 1, 1974; *Grand Prairie Daily News* (Grand Prairie, Texas), December 5, 1974; *Austin American-Statesman* (Austin, Texas), December 15, 1974.

[7] *St. Louis Post-Dispatch* (St. Louis, Missouri), February 2, 1974; *Mexico Ledger* (Mexico, Missouri), February 8, 1974; *The Decatur Herald* (Decatur, Illinois), February 10, 1974; *Hartford Courant* (Hartford, Connecticut), February 15, 1974; *The Philadelphia Inquirer* (Philadelphia, Pennsylvania), March 7, 1974; *The Greenville News* (Greenville, South Carolina), October 28, 1949.

[8] "Hamburger, with or without," *Chicago Tribune* (Chicago, Illinois), January 27, 1974.

[9] "Burger 'Birthplace' Faces Bulldozer," *The New York Times* (New York Times), January 12, 1974.

[10] "The Burger That Conquered the Country," *Time Magazine*, September 1973, 90.

[11] email exchange with author dated October 3, 2018.

[12] "German City is Not Home of Hamburger," *The Tribune* (Coshocton, Ohio), March 3, 1965; "Real Birth of Hamburger Took Place at 1904 Fair," *The Times Recorder* (Zanesville, Ohio), March 7, 1965; *Pensacola News Journal* (Pensacola, Florida), March 8, 1965; *Clarion-Ledger* (Jackson, Mississippi), March 10, 1965; *The Monitor* (McAllen, Texas), March 11, 1965; *The Daily News-Journal* (Murfreesboro, Tennessee), March 18, 1965; *The Odessa American* (Odessa, Texas), March 18, 1965; *Redlands Daily Facts* (Redlands, California), March 30, 1965; *Republican and Herald* (Pottsville, Pennsylvania), April 7, 1965; *Ames Daily Tribune* (Ames, Iowa), April 14, 1965; *The Press Democrat* (Santa Rosa,

California), June 29, 1965; *Bennington Banner* (Bennington, Vermont), July 1, 1965; *Anderson Herald* (Anderson, Indiana), September 4, 1965.

[13] John F. Love, *McDonald's: Behind the Arches* (New York: Bantam Books, 1995), 208.

[14] Neal O'Hara, "Pull Up a Chair," *The Greenville News* (Greenville, South Carolina), July 8, 1955.

[15] "Hamburger History," *Argus-Leader* (Sioux Falls, South Dakota), October 6, 1952.

[16] "This Ice Cream Cone Business a Sure Winner – Surprising Output of the St. Louis Exposition Dainty at Elwood Fair this Week," *Argus-Leader* (Sioux Falls, South Dakota), August 26, 1905. – "The ice cream cone, a feature of world's fair privilege at St. Louis, had its introduction to Elwood this week at the fair, and it was certainly a seller."

[17] "American Hamburger's 45th Anniversary To Be Celebrated Wednesday in Chicago," *Lubbock Evening Journal* (Lubbock, Texas), August 2, 1949.

[18] "Just 45 Years Ago Hamburgers Were Discovered," *The Daily Oklahoman* (Oklahoma City, Oklahoma), August 4, 1949.

[19] "Hamburger, US Developed, Now Celebrating 45th Birthday", *The Hutchinson News* (Hutchinson, Kansas), August 23, 1949; *The Times Recorder* (Zanesville, Ohio), August 26, 1949; *Clarion Ledger* (Jackson, Mississippi), August 26, 1949; *The Star Press* (Muncie, Indiana), August 28, 1949; *Journal and Courier* (Lafayette, Indiana), September 10, 1949; *Argus-Leader* (Sioux Falls, South Dakota), September 18, 1949; *The Greenville News* (Greenville, South Carolina), October 28, 1949,. [18"Hamburger, US Developed, Now Celebrating 45th Birthday", *The Hutchinson News* (Hutchinson, Kansas), August 23, 1949; *The Times Recorder* (Zanesville, Ohio), August 26, 1949; *Clarion Ledger* (Jackson, Mississippi), August 26, 1949; *The Star Press* (Muncie, Indiana), August 28, 1949; *Journal and Courier* (Lafayette, Indiana), September 10, 1949 *Argus-Leader* (Sioux Falls, South Dakota), September 18, 1949; *The Greenville News* (Greenville, South Carolina), October 28, 1949.

Chapter 14: A (Swiss) Cheesehead Tale

[1] Henry Otgaar, Corine de Ruiter, Mark L. Howe, Lisanne Hoetmer & Patricia van Reekum, "A Case Concerning Children's False Memories of Abuse: Recommendations Regarding Expert Witness Work," (2017), *Psychiatry, Psychology and Law, 24,* no. 3 (2017): 365-378.

[2] "Wanted," *The Capital Journal* (Salem, Oregon), September 13, 1909.

[3] Advertisement, *The Post-Crescent* (Appleton, Wisconsin), June 14, 1919.

[4] "Hamburger Charley to Celebrate Anniversary," *The Post-Crescent* (Appleton, Wisconsin), September 26, 1934.

[5] "Hamburger Charley to Celebrate Anniversary," *The Post-Crescent* (Appleton, Wisconsin), September 26, 1934.

[6] "Identity of Honest Man Learned After 49 Years," *The Post-Crescent* (Appleton, Wisconsin), October 25, 1934.

[7] "Identity of Honest Man Learned After 49 Years," *The Post-Crescent* (Appleton, Wisconsin), October 25, 1934.

[8] "A Notable Success – Seymour's First Annual Fair an Unprecedented Triumph," *Appleton Post*, October 15, 1885.

[9] "The Oshkosh fair will be held Sept 14 to 18," *The Neenah Daily Times* (Neenah, Wisconsin), March 24, 1885.

[10] "The New London Fair," *The Oshkosh Northwestern* (Oshkosh, Wisconsin), September 18, 1891.

[11] "Seymour Fair – Seymour's Fair, September 14th, 15th and 16th," *The Appleton Crescent* (Appleton, Wisconsin), September 12, 1891.

[12] "Races at the Fair... Oshkosh, September 22 to 25," *The Oshkosh Northwestern* (Oshkosh, Wisconsin), July 10, 1891.

[13] "Former Paint Company Head Dies Suddenly," *The Oshkosh Northwestern* (Oshkosh, Wisconsin), October 11, 1934.

Chapter 15: Marketing 101: Know Your Audience

[1] "Pioneer 'Hot Dog' Man and Originator of the Justly-Famous Ice Cream Cone, Tells of Catering to the Wants of Common People," *The Akron Beacon Journal* (Akron Ohio), September 15, 1922.

[2] Kerr, "Around the Town," *Akron Beacon Journal* (Akron, Ohio), December 6, 1938.

[3] Kerr, "Around the Town," *Akron Beacon Journal* (Akron, Ohio), December 5, 1938.

[4] Alec Burrell, "Off the Beaten Path – He Chose U.S. Career to Life as Swiss Watchmaker," *The Akron Beacon Journal* (Akron, Ohio), February 24, 1946.

[5] "Retail Prices," *The Akron Beacon Journal* (Akron, Ohio), March 23, 1892.

[6] Advertisement, *The Akron Beacon Journal* (Akron, Ohio), March 25, 1892.

[7] Notice, *Akron Evening Times* (Akron, Ohio), April 25, 1914.

[8] "Local Markets," *The Akron Beacon Journal* (Akron, Ohio), October 2, 1902.

[9] Kerr, "Around the Town," *Akron Beacon Journal* (Akron, Ohio), December 6, 1938.

[10] "Business Today – Hamburger Business Started In Akron," *The Akron Beacon Journal* (Akron, Ohio), November 5, 1939.

[11] Alec Burrell, "Off the Beaten Path – Daddy of Hamburger Sandwich? It's Akron's Mr. Frank Menches!" *The Akron Beacon Journal* (Akron, Ohio), April 20, 1948.

[12] "'Inventor' of Hamburger Dies," *Dayton Daily News* (Dayton, Ohio), October 5, 1951.

[13] "Retail Prices/Wholesale Prices," *The Akron Beacon Journal* (Akron, Ohio), September 23, 1885.

Chapter 16: CSI: Hamburg(er), N.Y.

[1] "Picnics," *Stark County Democrat* (Canton, Ohio), July 14, 1881.

[2] "A Field Day – Bicycle Races." *The Stark County Democrat* (Canton, Ohio), July 9, 1885.

[3] "The Salem Tournament," *The Stark County Democrat* (Canton, Ohio), July 8, 1886.

[4] "'Inventor' of Hamburger Dies," *Dayton Daily News* (Dayton, Ohio), October 5, 1951.

[5] Margaret Fess, "C-E Printer Writes Book on Circus Great," *Buffalo Courier-Express* (Buffalo, New York), August 19, 1964.

[6] Charles Menches is often cited with creating the Ice Cream Cone at the 1904 St. Louis World's Fair and in 1909 the Menches Brothers did receive a patent on the waffle cone iron they invented.

[7] "New Liberty Theater One of Finest; Has Both Beauty and Comfort," *The Akron Beacon Journal* (Akron, Ohio), September 8, 1921.

[8] "Stefos to Tell His Life Story Today," *The Kane Republican* (Kane, Pennsylvania), March 7, 1925.

[9] "Empire State News," *Buffalo Evening News* (Buffalo, New York), May 19, 1885.

[10] "Erie County Fair," *Erie County Independent* (Hamburg, New York), September 4, 1885.

[11] Letter dated June 17, 1985 to Supervisor Jack Quinn, Jr., re: "Hamburg Chamber of Commerce 'Birth of the Burger' Celebration"

[12] "The Fair at Hamburg – A Large Number of Entries and a Beautiful Display in Every Department. – Fair Weather and Good Attendance," *The Buffalo Commercial* (Buffalo, New York), September 17, 1885.

[13] "The Erie County Fair – An Average Attendance and Good Exhibits at Hamburg – Fine Stock Shown – Yesterday's Horse Races," *Buffalo Morning Express and Illustrated Buffalo Express* (Buffalo, New York), September 17, 1885.

[14] "Go and See Mollie Stark," *The Stark County Democrat* (Canton, Ohio), September 24, 1885.

[15] *The Democratic Press* (Ravenna, Ohio), October 8, 1885.

[16] John Menches and Ron Bush in discussion with the author, October 16, 2017.

[17] "The County Fair," *Buffalo Morning Express and Illustrated Buffalo Express* (Buffalo, New York), September 23, 1884.

[18] "Erie County Agricultural Society," *Erie County Independent* (Hamburg, New York), October 10, 1884.

[19] "Reports of Standing Committees," *The Buffalo Commercial* (Buffalo, New York), February 3, 1891.

[20] June Streamer, "Popular Hamburg Sandwich to Receive a Two-Day Salut on Its 100th Anniversary," *Hamburg Sun* (Hamburg, New York), July 25, 1985.

[21] "The Village of Hamburg – A Brief Description of its Business and Institutions of Public Interest," *Springville Journal* (East Aurora, New York), July 24, 1875.

[22] "Hamburg," *The Buffalo Times* (Buffalo, New York), April 1, 1889.

[23] "The Erie County Fair," *Springville Journal* (East Aurora, New York), September 27, 1873.

[24] "Erie County Supervisors," *Buffalo Morning Express and Illustrated Buffalo Express* (Buffalo, New York), October 10, 1877.

[25] "The Fair," *Erie County Independent* (Hamburg, New York), September 25, 1885.

[26] "Local Observations – September 18, 1885," *Buffalo Morning Express* (Buffalo, New York), September 19, 1885.

[27] "Fun at the Fair – Hamburg the Center of Attraction for Erie County People – How the Politician Works It – A Comparison with Previous Fairs – 10,000 People Expected There Today," *The Buffalo Times* (Buffalo, New York), September 17, 1885.

[28] "Erie County Fair," *Erie County Independent* (Hamburg, New York), August 7, 1885.

[29] "Hamburg's Gala Day – Over 3,000 Buffalonians at the Fair Yesterday. – The Crowd Estimated at 10,000 – Lively Races and Splendid Exhibits," *The Buffalo Commercial* (Buffalo, New York), September 18, 1885.

[30] "Dairying," *Springville Journal* (East Aurora, New York), March 13, 1880.

Chapter 17: A Day in Hamburger History – September 18, 1885

[1] As in Chapter 1, much of this retelling can be sources contemporary newspapers. In some cases, we rely on secondary sources. Where the sources run dry, we extrapolate from these sources as best we could. – Author

Epilogue: A Family Rediscovers Itself

[1] Matters pertaining to Menches family based on several interviews with Judy Kusmits, Ron Bush, and John Menches. Matters pertaining to the 1985 Hamburg Chamber of Commerce event based on an interview with Esther Kowal, Librarian at Frontier Central School District.

INDEX:

ABOUT THE AUTHOR

Christopher Carosa is a popular and entertaining speaker who has appeared from coast to coast. As an award-winning financial writer, his thoughts and opinions have been sought out by such major media outlets as *The Wall Street Journal*, *The New York Times*, *USA Today*, *Barron's*, CNBC, CNN, and Fox Business News. But his work isn't limited to money talk. A long-time newspaper columnist writing on everything from white cream donuts to international geopolitics, he's been recognized by the New York Press Association for his editorial writing. In 2018, he was elected president of the National Society of Newspaper Columnists.

Mr. Carosa has accumulated a long, variegated, and successful record as a practitioner in the financial services industry. After earning a degree in physics and astronomy from Yale University in 1982, he joined a small regional investment adviser. While there, he earned his MBA from the Simon School at the University of Rochester and the CTFA (Certified Trust and Financial Adviser) professional designation from the Institute of Certified Bankers.

In 1989, he founded a weekly community newspaper when his hometown paper abruptly and unexpectedly folded. He sold that paper to fund the start-up of Carosa Stanton Asset Management, LLC, a boutique investment firm where he serves as president. He's also Chairman of the Board and President of Bullfinch Fund, Inc. a series of flexible no-load mutual funds, including one that concentrates its investments in Western New York companies. His wife eventually re-acquired the newspaper and Mr. Carosa has returned to his old position as publisher and columnist.

If you'd like to read more by Mr. Carosa, feel free to browse his author's site, ChrisCarosa.com; LifetimeDreamGuide.com, a site to another book he's working on; his site devoted to his first love, AstronomyTop100.com; and, TheMacaroniKid.com, a musical/comedy stage play he wrote that has played to sold-out community theater crowds. Not bad for a Physics and Astronomy major.

Mr. Carosa lives in Mendon, NY with his wife, Betsy, three children, Cesidia, Catarina, and Peter, and their beagle, Wally.

Made in the USA
Middletown, DE
22 December 2018